100
Trivia Quizzes
for
Stamp Collectors

by Bill Olcheski

1982
American Philatelic Society

Introduction

Trivia quizzes are fun. They add interest to stamp club meetings in addition to furthering knowledge of stamps and the nations that issue them.

The quizzes in this book cover the stamps of the United States and those of many foreign countries. There also are general information quizes on stamp collecting.

The quizzes are graded as to difficulty and appropriate point values are assigned to the various questions. Some are easy and will elicit quick answers from the newest of collectors. Other questions will challenge the memory and knowledge of even the most advanced.

To use the book at a club meeting, divide the group into teams placing both experienced and inexperienced collectors on each team. Designate a quizmaster and a scorekeeper. The special interests of club members can serve as a guide to which quizzes are used. Set a time limit on the program to maintain maximum interest.

Philatelic prizes should be awarded to the winners.

The more you know about stamps the more you will enjoy the hobby. Stamp collecting is meant to be fun. Introducing the element of competition through these quizzes will make it easier to reach that goal. Happy collecting!

— Bill Olcheski

For Rosemary
. . . I couldn't make it without you.

Contents

6

United States Stamps

Quiz No. 1

Five Point Questions

1. The 200th anniversary of what university is marked by a 1954 stamp?
2. What is the denomination of the stamps in the Overrun Countries series of 1943-44?
3. What ship is shown on a three-cent commemorative issued in 1947?
4. What Indian appears on the five-cent stamp in the Jamestown Exposition set?

Ten-Point Questions

5. What sport is featured on a U.S. envelope issued in 1971?
6. What is shown on the 80-cent airmail stamp of 1952?
7. What do all U.S. issues from 1847 to 1894 have in common?

Twenty-Five Point Questions

8. What U.S. President appears on a five-cent stamp issued in 1875?
9. What was the last year in which Hawaii issued its own stamps?

Fifty-Point Question

10. Who is the artist who appears on the five-cent stamp in the 1940 Famous American series?

Quiz No. 2

Five-Point Questions

1. What is the denomination of the stamp with the famous inverted airplane?
2. What woman fliers are the subject of U.S. airmail stamps?
3. What President appears on an eleven-cent airmail envelope of 1965?
4. What pioneer is shown on the Kentucky statehood issue of 1942?

Ten-Point Questions

5. In what year did the U.S. issue a stamp marking the landing of the Swedes and Finns in America?
6. Three children appear on a four-cent stamp of 1959. What are they promoting?
7. On the Century of Progress issue of 1933, what fort is shown on the one-cent stamp?

Twenty-Five Point Questions

8. In what year was the Golden Gate Exposition held in San Francisco?
9. What color are the special handling stamps of 1925?

Fifty-Point Question

10. What animal is shown on the Nebraska statehood stamp of 1967?

Quiz No. 3

Five-Point Questions

1. How many souvenir sheets make up the Bicentennial issue of 1976?
2. The skyline of what city is shown on the 1951 stamp marking the landing of Cadillac?
3. Labor Leader Samuel Gompers was the subject of a 1950 stamp. What was its denomination?
4. What color is the Edith Wharton 15-cent stamp of 1980?

Ten-Point Questions

5. Who appears on the five-dollar stamp of the 1938 definitive series?
6. What sport is featured on a 1978 U.S. envelope?
7. What is the denomination of the only registry stamp issued by the United States?

Twenty-Five Point Questions

8. What two people are shown on the four-dollar Columbian issue?
9. The Sokols are honored on a 1965 issue. What is their area of special interest?

Fifty-Point Question

10. What is shown on the air post special delivery stamps of 1934?

Quiz No. 4

Five-Point Questions

1. What was the denomination of the first U.S. airmail stamp?
2. Whose flight is honored on a ten-cent airmail stamp of 1927?
3. What type ship is shown on the three-cent issue of 1946?
4. How many stamps are there in the National Capital Sesquicentennial issue of 1950?

Ten-Point Questions

5. In the 1940 Famous American set honoring poets what is the denomation of the James Whitcomb Riley stamp?
6. What branch of the Armed Forces is honored on a five-cent postal card issued in 1968?
7. What color was the Champion of Liberty four-cent stamp honoring Mahatma Gandhi?

Twenty-Five Point Questions

8. Who is on the twenty-five-cent stamp of the 1938 definitives?
9. In what year were stamped envelopes first issued in the U.S.?

Fifty-Point Question

10. In the 1975-79 definitive series, what appears on the two-dollar stamp?

Quiz No. 5

Five-Point Questions

1. A 1980 issue features a juggler. Who is he?
2. What two denominations did the Champion of Liberty stamps use?
3. What is the nationality of the ship shown on a three-cent stamp issued in 1953 to mark the founding of New York?
4. How many stamps were there in the 1974 set marking the centenary of the Universal Postal Union?

Ten-Point Questions

5. In the 1940 Famous Americans what is the denomination of the John Greenleaf Whittier stamp?
6. What tree is featured on the Connecticut Tercentenary issue of 1935?
7. The U.S. issued a stamp for the Philippines in 1934. What sport was shown on the two-cent stamp?

Twenty-Five Point Questions

8. Whose painting of the Virgin and Child appears on the 1979 Christmas issue?
9. In what year did the U.S. issue four Christmas stamps showing toys?

Fifty-Point Question

10. What playwright appears on the one-dollar stamp of The Prominent Americans issue of 1965-78?

Quiz No. 6

Five-Point Questions

1. What American folk art is the subject of a 1978 series?
2. What sport is shown on the Olympic Games airmail issue of 1972?
3. What was the name of the Russian spacecraft shown on the 1975 U.S. ten-cent stamp?
4. What birds appear on the wildlife conservation issue of 1957?

Ten-Point Questions

5. How many different windmills appear on the booklet panes of 15-cent stamps issued in 1980?
6. What are the denominations of the stamps in the Lincoln Sesquicentennial issue of 1958-59?
7. What scientist appears on the 10-cent stamp in the Famous American series of 1940?

Twenty-Five Point Questions

8. What airplane is shown on the twenty-five-cent Trans-Pacific issue of 1935?
9. In what year was a stamp issued marking the centennial of Oregon statehood?

Fifty-Point Question

10. Whose gun battery appears on the Battle of White Plains stamp of 1926?

Quiz No. 7

Five-Point Questions

1. Whose portrait appears on the Bicentennial stamps of 1932?
2. Who is on the one-cent value of the 1938 definitives?
3. A cable car from what city is shown on the Historic Preservation stamps of 1971?
4. What British statesman appears on a five-cent 1965 issue?

Ten-Point Questions

5. What scientist appears on the two-cent stamp in the Famous Americans series?
6. What type Olympic athlete is shown on the twenty-one-cent airmail postal card of 1979?
7. Who appears on the five-dollar stamp of 1894?

Twenty-Five Point Questions

8. What was the highest denomination of Postal Note stamps issued in 1945?
9. What famous movie maker appeared on a 1975 commemorative?

Fifty-Point Question

10. What occupation is depicted on the 1-cent U.S. Parcel Post stamp of 1912?

Quiz No. 8

Five-Point Questions

1. Who is on the three-cent value of the 1938 definitives?
2. What American boy is shown on the Folklore stamp of 1972?
3. How many stamps are there in the American Credo series of 1960-61?
4. Who is the scientist honored on a 1964 airmail issue?

Ten-Point Questions

5. What Polish astronomer is shown on a 1973 stamp?
6. What color were the parcel post postage due stamps of 1912?
7. What scientist appears on the one-cent stamp in the Famous American series?

Twenty-Five Point Questions

8. The U.S. issued a 16-cent stamp for the Philippines in 1934. What sport did it show?
9. What bird appears on the one-dollar airlift stamp of 1968?

Fifty-Point Question

10. In what year were Christmas seals first introduced?

Quiz No. 9

Five-Point Questions

1. What famous yacht race is the subject of a 1980 U.S. envelope?
2. How many stamps are there in the Overrun Countries set of 1943-44?
3. Who is on the ten-cent stamp of the 1938 definitives?
4. Eli Whitney invented the cotton gin. On what denomination stamp is he honored?

Ten-Point Questions

5. What foreign monument is shown on a U.S. issue of 1945?
6. Augustus Saint-Gaudens appears on a three-cent stamp. In what year was it issued?
7. What flower appears on the Alabama statehood issue of 1969?

Twenty-Five Point Questions

8. In the Famous American series what is the color of the stamp showing Mark Hopkins?
9. Who is on the two-dollar stamp of the 1938 definitives?

Fifty-Point Question

10. What year was the use of rotary press printing introduced for engraved U.S. stamps?

Quiz No. 10

Five-Point Questions

1. How many stamps are there in the historic flag series of 1968?
2. On what denomination stamp does Stephen Collins Foster appear?
3. Who is on the six-cent value in the 1938 definitives?
4. What humorist was the subject of a 1948 issue?

Ten-Point Questions

5. What is the denomination of the stamp issued in 1937 showing the seal of the Naval Academy and two Midshipmen?
6. In what year was the stamp showing the Iwo Jima flag raising issued?
7. On the Louisiana Purchase issue of 1904, who is shown on the five-cent stamp?

Twenty-Five Point Questions

8. In the Americana issue of 1975-79, what three objects are on the four-cent stamp?
9. What former postmaster general appears on an air-mail stamp?

Fifty-Point Question

10. When was the 1847 issue of U.S. stamps declared invalid for use as postage?

Quiz No. 11

Five-Point Questions

1. Lajos Kossuth was honored as a Champion of Liberty. From what country did he come?
2. How many stamps were there in the postal note issue of 1945?
3. Who is on the thirty-cent stamp in the 1938 definitives?
4. What was the former name of the U.S. Virgin Islands?

Ten-Point Questions

5. In the Famous American series, what is the denomination of the James Russell Lowell stamp?
6. What anniversary of the adoption of Christianity in Poland is marked by a U.S. stamp?
7. In what year did the U.S. issue a stamp showing a Light Brahma Rooster?

Twenty-Five Pint Questions

8. What author appears on the two-cent Famous American stamp?
9. What U.S. ambassador to the United Nations appears on a 1965 stamp?

Fifty-Point Questions

10. What three people are shown on the Confederate Memorial Stamp of 1970?

Quiz No. 12

Five-Point Questions

1. If Whistler wanted a stamp with a picture of his mother, what would it have cost in 1934?
2. Alexander Graham Bell appears on a ten-cent stamp. Does he have a beard?
3. How many stamps were there in the 1964 Christmas issue?
4. Who is on the one-dollar value in the 1938 definitives?

Ten-Point Questions

5. What flower appears on the Mississippi statehood stamp of 1967?
6. What author appears on the ten-cent Famous Americans stamp?
7. In what year did the U.S. issue its first Red Cross commemorative?

Twenty-Five Point Questions

8. What is the color of the 1940 stamp showing Charles W. Eliot?
9. In what year was the World's Fair held in New York?

Fifty-Point Question

10. What kind of birds are shown on the John James Audubon issue of 1963?

Quiz No. 13

Five-Point Questions

1. Noah Webster appears on a 1958 commemorative. What kind of books did he write?
2. Who is on the five-cent 1938 definitive?
3. What scientist appears on the five-cent stamp in the Famous American series?
4. How many stamps appear on the 1956 FIPEX sheet?

Ten-Point Questions

5. What famous artist's daughter appears on a 1965 five-cent stamp?
6. Victor Herbert appears on a three-cent stamp. In what year was it issued?
7. How much did it cost to send a single-sheet letter up to 300 miles in 1845?

Twenty-Five Point Questions

8. How many children are shown on the 1979 Year of the Child stamp?
9. What is the highest denomination in the parcel post stamps of 1912?

Fifty-Point Question

10. What ship appears on the shipbuilding issue of 1957?

Quiz No. 14

Five-Point Questions

1. When did the Philippines become independent and begin issuing their own stamps?
2. Who is on the seven-cent definitive of 1938?
3. On what denomination stamp does inventor Elias Howe appear?
4. Who is shown on the thirteen-cent stamp of the Prominent American series of 1965-78?

Ten-Point Questions

5. What explorer is shown on the one-cent stamp issued for use in Cuba under U.S. military rule in 1899?
6. Stamp collecting is honored on a stamp. In what year was it issued?
7. A sentry box at Morro Castle appears on a 1971 issue. Where is Morro Castle?

Twenty-Five Point Questions

8. What is the color of the stamp honoring Frances E. Willard in the Famous Educator series?
9. The Christmas stamps of 1970 showed four toys. What are they?

Fifty-Point Question

10. What ship appears on the 1944 steamship issue?

Quiz No. 15

Five-Point Questions

1. What type of transportation is shown on a fifteen-cent envelope issue of 1980?
2. What country was honored on the first stamp in the Overrun Countries series?
3. Who is on the eleven-cent definitive of 1938?
4. How many stamps are there in the butterfly issue of 1977?

Ten-Point Questions

5. In what year was the Alaska statehood airmail issued?
6. The creator of "Porgy and Bess" appears on a 1973 stamp. Who is he?
7. What is the child doing on the Special Olympics stamp of 1979?

Twenty-Five Point Questions

8. What park is featured on the eight-cent value of the National Parks series of 1934?
9. What Arizona plant appears on the statehood issue of 1962?

Fifty-Point Question

10. What two birds appear on stamps in the wildlife conservation issue of 1972?

Quiz No. 16

Five-Point Questions

1. Whose log cabin appears on a 1956 commemorative?
2. Who appears on the one-dollar stamp of the 1954 Liberty series?
3. Where were the Olympic Games held in 1932?
4. What is the shape of the indicia design on the 1956 FIPEX postal card?

Ten-Point Questions

5. Which amendment to the Constitution is commemorated on the Susan B. Anthony stamp?
6. What is the highest denomination in the 1934 National Parks series?
7. In what year was the Hawaii statehood airmail issued?

Twenty-Five Point Questions

8. Who is on the nineteen-cent stamp in the 1938 definitives?
9. What body of water appears on a 1972 airmail postal card?

Fifty-Point Question

10. In the definitive series of 1975-79, what appears on a five-dollar stamp?

Quiz No. 17

Five-Point Questions

1. How many stamps are there in the Franklin D. Roosevelt Memorial issue of 1945?
2. The canalization of what river is the subject of a 1929 issue?
3. The Kansas state flower appears on the statehood issue of 1961. What is it?
4. What sport is saluted in the James A. Naismith issue of 1961?

Ten-Point Questions

5. What is on the four and one-half cent 1938 definitive?
6. What newspaper publisher was honored on a three-cent stamp in 1948?
7. What presidential candidate appears on a 1945 issue?

Twenty-Five Point Questions

8. On which of the Overrun Countries stamps is there an error?
9. What woman author is honored on a five-cent 1940 stamp?

Fifty-Point Question

10. Whose statue is on the Rough Riders issue of 1948?

Quiz No. 18

Five-Point Questions

1. Who appeared on the first stamp in the Champion of Liberty series?
2. What inventor is shown with his chest covered with medals on a 1940 stamp?
3. What type of postal service is honored on a five-cent stamp issued in 1963?
4. How many stamps are there in the state flags issue of 1976?

Ten-Point Questions

5. What is the denomination of the stamp showing composer Edward A. McDowell?
6. What government agency is honored on an eight-cent stamp issued in 1972?
7. The first Kentucky settlement was honored with a stamp in 1974. Where was it?

Twenty-Five Point Questions

8. What ship appears on the two-cent value in the Norse-American set of 1925?
9. Who is honored as the organizer of the first volunteer firemen in America?

Fifty-Point Question

10. Three Thomas A. Edison stamps were issued in 1929. How can you tell them apart?

Quiz No. 19

Five-Point Questions

1. What slogan appeared on a three-cent stamp issued in 1942?
2. What famous battle is honored by a souvenir sheet issued in 1926?
3. Who is on the two-cent value of the 1938 definitives?
4. Adolph S. Ochs was the subject of a 1976 stamp. Of what newspaper was he the publisher?

Ten-Point Questions

5. How many children are shown on the family planning stamp of 1972?
6. The Sandy Hook Lighthouse appears on a twenty-nine-cent stamp in the Americana series. In what state is it located?
7. How many stamps are there on the 1978 CAPEX souvenir sheet?

Twenty-Five Point Questions

8. What is the occupation of the woman shown on the Skilled Hands for Independence stamp of 1977?
9. What method of transportation is shown on the twenty-cent parcel post stamp of 1912?

Fifty-Point Question

10. The purchase of the Alaska-Yukon territory from the Russians was marked by a stamp issued in 1909. Whose picture is on it?

Quiz No. 20

Five-Point Questions

1. William Penn was honored on a 1932 stamp. Of what religious group was he a member?
2. Who is on the one and one-half cent 1938 definitive?
3. What first lady appears on a four-cent stamp in the 1923 regular issue?
4. What Polish hero appears on a five-cent stamp issued in 1933?

Ten-Point Questions

5. What was the denomination of the petroleum industry issue of 1959?
6. What jazz musician is honored on a 1969 stamp?
7. What disease does a 1965 five-cent stamp crusade against?

Twenty-Five Point Questions

8. What color is the 1940 stamp honoring Ethelbert Nevin?
9. What four freedoms are covered in the 1943 issue?

Fifty-Point Question

10. Montgomery Blair appears on a 1963 airmail issue. Under what President was he postmaster general?

Quiz No. 21

Five-Point Questions

1. Which was issued first, the Harry Truman stamp or the Lyndon B. Johnson stamp?
2. What photographic inventor is shown on a 1954 issue?
3. What Alaska mountain appears on the fifteen 1-cent stamp in the National Park series?
4. What President appears on a two-cent stamp issued for the Canal Zone in 1949?

Ten-Point Questions

5. Who is on the fourteen-cent 1938 definitive?
6. In what year did the U.S. adopt adhesive stamps?
7. The Battle of Yorktown is the subject of a 1981 stamp. In what other year was a Battle of Yorktown stamp issued?

Twenty-Five Point Questions

8. What color is the 1940 stamp showing Booker T. Washington?
9. Who is on the eighteen-cent stamp of the 1938 definitives?

Fifty-Point Question

10. Who appears on both the two-dollar and the five-dollar stamps of 1918?

Quiz No. 22

Five-Point Questions

1. On August 15, 1947, a stamp was issued in Bath, Maine. What industry did it honor?
2. In what year did the U.S. end domestic airmail service?
3. "Old Faithful" appears on a 1972 commemorative. In what national park is it located?
4. What animal appears on the thirty-cent definitive of 1922-25?

Ten-Point Questions

5. Who is on the twelve-cent 1938 definitive?
6. What athletic activity is depicted on the 1979 Olympic postal card?
7. What are the denominations of the Graf Zeppelin issue?

Twenty-Five Point Questions

8. What author appears on the three-cent stamp in the Famous American series?
9. What is the name of the lamp shown on the fifty-cent stamp in the Americana issue of 1975-79?

Fifty-Point Question

10. What vehicle is shown on the ten-cent special delivery stamp of 1922?

Quiz No. 23

Five-Point Questions

1. The U.S. issued a series of stamps in 1934 which came to be known as "Farley's Follies." What was the subject of the series?
2. What American President appears on a 1964 commemorative?
3. Toleware from what state is shown on the 1979 American Folk Art issue?
4. Cordell Hull is shown on a 1963 commemorative. What was his job?

Ten-Point Questions

5. Fort Snelling appears on a 1970 anniversary stamp. In what state is it located?
6. Who is on the twenty-cent 1938 definitive?
7. What is the denomination of the Palace of Governors issue of 1960?

Twenty-Five Point Questions

8. What method of transportation is shown on the five-cent parcel post stamps of 1912?
9. In the Famous American series of 1940, what is the color of the Horace Mann stamp?

Fifty-Point Question

10. What four areas are singled out for beautification series of six-cent stamps?

Quiz No. 24

Five-Point Questions

1. What flower appears on the Alabama statehood stamp?
2. Who is on the 1938 eight-cent definitive?
3. What was the denomination of the airlift stamp of 1968?
4. Who appears on the five-cent stamp of the first issue of 1847?

Ten-Point Questions

5. The U.S. issued a six-cent stamp for the Philippines in 1934. What sport did it show?
6. Two people are shown on the 1969 football stamp. One is a player, what is the other?
7. Who is on the fifty-cent value of the 1938 definitives?

Twenty-Five Point Questions

8. In what year did the U.S. honor Susan B. Anthony by issuing a stamp showing her portrait?
9. Cyrus Hall McCormick invented the reaper. What is the color of the stamp issued in his honor?

Fifty-Point Question

10. In what year were encased postage stamps introduced?

Quiz No. 25

Five-Point Questions

1. The discovery of what body of water is commemorated on a ten-cent stamp in the Panama Pacific Exposition issue of 1913?
2. What American President appears on the 1942 stamp honoring the resistance by the Chinese people to aggression from Japan?
3. In the Famous American Series, what is the denomination of the Henry Wadsworth Longfellow stamp?
4. Who is on the sixteen-cent stamp in the 1938 definitives?

Ten-Point Questions

5. What Ohio Senator appears on a 1960 commemorative?
6. What is the shape of the stamp on the eight-cent airmail envelope of 1962?
7. What building appears on the one and one-quarter cent definitive of 1954?

Twenty-Five Point Questions

8. The John Sloan issue of 1970 features one of his paintings. Which one?
9. Old North Church appears on a stamp in the Americana Series. What is its denomination?

Fifty-Point Question

10. In what year did the postmaster of New York begin using his own adhesive stamps called "Postmasters' Provisionals?"

Quiz No. 26

Five-Point Questions

1. What anniversary of the claiming of Louisiana was marked by a 1982 postal card?
2. How many stamps are there in the July 4, 1976 Declaration of Independence issue?
3. What flower is shown on the Mississippi statehood stamp?
4. In what city was the 1956 International Philatelic Exhibition held?

Ten-Point Questions

5. Who is on the seventeen-cent stamp of the 1938 definitives?
6. Who is shown with Virginia Dare on the 1937 commemorative?
7. In what year did artist Gilbert Charles Stuart appear on a U.S. stamp?

Twenty-Five Point Questions

8. A mosaic from the headquarters of what labor group is shown on the 1956 Labor Day issue?
9. What animal was featured on a U.S. envelope issued in 1970?

Fifty-Point Question

10. What scientist appears on the three-cent stamp in the Famous American Series?

Quiz No. 27

Five-Point Questions

1. What is the denomination of the only certified mail stamp issued by the U.S.?
2. A stamp honoring the World's Fair was issued in 1962. In what city was the fair held?
3. The Alamo appears on a nine-cent stamp issued in 1956. In what city is it located?
4. The originator of the Memorial Poppy appears on a 1948 stamp. Who is she?

Ten-Point Questions

5. What is the central design feature of the airmail set issued for the Canal Zone in 1951?
6. What ship appears on the fourteen-cent postal card of 1978?
7. What is the denomination of the bulk mail stamp showing a drum?

Twenty-Five Point Questions

8. What type vessel is shown on the International Naval Review stamp of 1957?
9. What American couple appears on the paid reply postal card of 1951?

Fifty-Point Question

10. When did the U.S. stop issuing stamps for Cuba?

Quiz No. 28

Five-Point Questions

1. What was the name of President Theodore Roosevelt's house that appeared on a 1953 stamp?
2. What animal appears on the stamp honoring the Humane Society?
3. What is the denomination of the Walt Whitman stamp in the 1940 series?
4. What is shown on the New Hampshire stamp of 1955?

Ten-Point Questions

5. In what city was the HemisFair of 1968 held?
6. What ship is shown on the Four Chaplains issue of 1948?
7. Who is on the twenty-two-cent value of the 1938 definitives?

Twenty-Five Point Questions

8. The U.S. issued two stamps for the Xth Olympiad in 1932. What did the designs show?
9. What color are the windmill stamps in the 1980 booklets?

Fifty-Point Questions

10. What Revolutionary War patriot is shown on the one-cent value of the Louisiana Purchase stamps of 1904?

Quiz No. 29

Five-Point Questions

1. The U.S. issued its first "self-adhesive" stamp in 1974. What did it show?
2. What color is the Diamond Head eighty-cent airmail of 1952?
3. Thomas G. Masaryk appears on two 1960 stamps. From what country did he come?
4. The fleet of Columbus is shown on one of the 1893 Columbian issues. What was the denomination?

Ten-Point Questions

5. How many stamps are there in the CAPEX souvenir sheet of 1978?
6. What type writing instrument is shown on the Religious Freedom issue of 1957?
7. How many stars are there on the four-cent flag stamp isued in 1959?

Twenty-Five Point Questions

8. Who is on the twenty-cent stamp of the 1938 definitive set?
9. How many stamps are there in the Columbian Exposition issue of 1893?

Fifty-Point Question

10. What is the name of the ship on the one-cent value in the Huguenot-Walloon issue of 1924?

Quiz No. 30

Five-Point Questions

1. What fictional character appears on the 1974 issue for the Legend of Sleepy Hollow?
2. What President appears on a twenty-five-cent airmail stamp issued in 1960?
3. Who is on the one-half cent value of the 1938 definitives?
4. What was the color of the Thomas Edison stamps of 1929?

Ten-Point Questions

5. What famous publisher and editor was the subject of a 1961 commemorative?
6. In what year did the U.S. issue a stamp to mark the 100th anniversary of the California Gold Rush?
7. What was the denomination of the George Rogers Clark stamp of 1929?

Twenty-Five Point Questions

8. The 1956 wildlife conservation issue showed three types of wildlife. Name them.
9. What explorer appears on the one-cent stamp of the Panama-Pacific issue of 1913?

Fifty-Point Question

10. A Washington, D.C. buidling now used as a museum appears as one stamp in the Historic Preservation issue of 1971. What is it?

Quiz No. 31

Five-Point Questions

1. An airmail postal card was issued in 1967 for the Boy Scout World Jamboree. What was the denomination?
2. Ramon Magsaysay appeared on the first Champion of Liberty stamp. From what country did he come?
3. The 100th anniversary of what kind of business is marked by a 1927 stamp?
4. What author is shown on the one-cent stamp in the Famous Americans Series?

Ten-Point Questions

5. The first automated post office in the U.S. was the subject of a 1960 stamp. Where was it?
6. What is the athlete doing on the professional baseball stamp of 1969?
7. Edgar Lee Masters appears on a 1970 commemorative. What was his claim to fame?

Twenty-Five Point Questions

8. On the Trans-Mississippi issue of 1898, what is shown on the eight-cent stamp?
9. What kinds of cattle are shown on the eight-cent Rural America stamp of 1973?

Fifty-Point Question

10. The "Swamp Fox of the Carolinas" was honored on a 1982 postal card. Who was he?

Quiz No. 32

Five-Point Questions

1. Ignacy Jan Paderewski is the subject of a 1960 stamp. What musical instrument did he play.
2. The first man to land on the moon appears on a ten-cent stamp of 1969. Who is he?
3. The 200th anniversary of diplomatic relations with what country was marked in 1982?
4. Giuseppe Garibaldi appears on the 1960 Champion of Liberty stamps. From what country did he come?

Ten-Point Questions

5. The first airmail flights came in 1918. Between what two cities did they go?
6. A five-cent commemorative marked the 300th anniversary of the colonization of an eastern state. Which state was it?
7. "Breezing Up" is featured on a 1962 stamp. Who painted it?

Twenty-Five Point Questions

8. What U.S. issue of 1901 signalled the dawning of the industrial age?
9. Who is on the twenty-one-cent stamp of the 1938 definitive set?

Fifty-Point Question

10. Many famous artists perform in an amphitheater outside of Washington, D.C. It appears on a six-cent stamp. What is it?

Quiz No. 33

Five-Point Questions

1. The Iwo Jima Memorial appears on a 1945 stamp. In what city is it?
2. Whose picture appears on the first Confederate stamp?
3. What sport is shown on the Lake Placid Olympic issue of 1932?
4. What anniversary of football was marked by a 1969 stamp?

Ten-Point Questions

5. The World's Fair in what city was the subject of a 1958 stamp?
6. In what year were the first U.S. Christmas stamps issued?
7. A 1949 airmail marks the 200th anniversary of what American city?

Twenty-Five Point Questions

8. A stamp issued in 1955 showing the Great Lakes and two steamers marked what event?
9. What is shown on the Canal Zone postage dues of 1932-41?

Fifty-Point Question

10. The Missouri Sesquicentennial issue featured a painting called "Independence and the Opening of the West." Who was the artist?

Quiz No. 34

Five-Point Questions

1. In what year was a stamp issued honoring the Library of Congress?
2. Gustaf Mannerheim appears on a 1960 set. From what country did he come?
3. Mount McKinley is the subject of a fifteen-cent stamp issued in 1972. Where is it located?
4. What two sports appear on stamps issued in 1969?

Ten-Point Questions

5. What painter is on the ten-cent stamp in the Famous American Series?
6. How many stamps are there in the American Quilts issue of 1978?
7. What is the denomination of the 1949 airmail stamp honoring the Wright Brothers?

Twenty-Five Point Questions

8. The Battle of New Orleans anniversary rated a stamp in 1965. In what year was it fought?
9. Harlan Fiske Stone was the subject of a 1948 stamp. What was his job?

Fifty-Point Question

10. Virginia Dare appears on a 1937 stamp marking the settlement of which American colony?

Quiz No. 35

Five-Point Questions

1. What building appears on the ten-cent stamp in the 1954 Liberty Series?
2. What famous bandmaster appears on a 1940 issue?
3. The independence of what country is marked by a 1960 commemorative?
4. Guttenberg was commemorated for printing of the first book. What was it?

Ten-Point Questions

5. What sport is featured on a 1974 U.S. envelope?
6. How many sheep appear on the stamp honoring the American Wool Industry in 1971?
7. What was the denomination of the postal card honoring the U.S. Coast Guard in 1965?

Twenty-Five Point Questions

8. A Washington Irving story was the inspiration for a 1974 stamp. What was it?
9. What color is the five-dollar Alexander Hamilton stamp of 1956?

Fifty-Point Question

10. What ship appears on the twelve-cent stamp of 1869?

Quiz No. 36

Five-Point Questions

1. What poet is shown on an eight-cent stamp of 1971?
2. How many stars are on the flag stamp issued in 1968?
3. Who is on the four-cent value of the 1938 definitives?
4. Simon Bolivar was on a 1958 stamp. From what country does he come?

Ten-Point Questions

5. The man who served as Secretary of State longer than any other is on a 1963 stamp. Who is he?
6. A block of four stamps saluted the 1982 World's Fair. Where was it held?
7. The President of what country was featured on the first Champion of Liberty stamp?

Twenty-Five Point Questions

8. What was the denomination of the 1965 stamp honoring the International Telecommunications Union?
9. Sidney Lanier appeared on a 1972 stamp. What was his occupation?

Fifty-Point Question

10. When the five-cent James Monroe stamp was issued in 1954, what was the first day city?

Quiz No. 37

Five-Point Questions

1. A stamp showing a desert scene was issued in 1962. The 50th anniversary of what state does it honor?
2. What was the denomination of the stamps in the Historic Flag Series of 1968?
3. What anniversay of baseball was marked by a 1969 stamp?
4. Who is on the fifteen-cent stamp of the 1938 definitives?

Ten-Point Questions

5. The 100th anniversary of friendship between what two countries is marked by a stamp issued in 1948?
6. Monticello is featured on a twenty-cent stamp of 1956. Of what President was it the home?
7. When the 1972 stamp was issued marking the inauguration of the U.S. Postal Service, what was the first day city?

Twenty-Five Point Questions

8. In what city was an Urban Planning Stamp issued in 1967?
9. What 1862 law was the subject of a 1962 stamp?

Fifty-Point Question

10. In what year were the first postal cards issued?

Quiz No. 38

Five-Point Questions

1. What vehicle is shown on a two-cent coil issued in 1982?
2. The inventor of basketball was honored on a 1961 stamp. Who was he?
3. On the one-cent stamp issued in 1959 does Lincoln have a beard?
4. Who is on the nine-cent definitive of 1938?

Ten-Point Questions

5. What was the denomination of the postal card honoring the U.S. Customs Service in 1964?
6. In what city was the 1965 Churchill stamp issued?
7. How many stamps are there in the American Trees issue of 1978?

Twenty-Five Point Questions

8. Nassau Hall is shown on a 1956 stamp. Of what school is it a part?
9. The "Minute Man" statue appears on a stamp issued in 1925. What was the denomination?

Fifty-Point Question

10. In what city was the Rotary International stamp of 1955 issued?

Quiz No. 39

Five-Point Questions

1. What famous railroad engineer appears on a U.S. stamp?
2. Mahatma Gandhi appears on a 1961 stamp. From what country does he come?
3. What color is the certified mail stamp of 1955?
4. In what year did the first U.S. stamps without denomination appear?

Ten-Point Questions

5. Who appears on the two-dollar definitive of 1918?
6. Which ship of Columbus appears on the three-cent issue of 1893?
7. King Kamehameha IV appears on the stamps of a kingdom that eventually became a state. Which is it?

Twenty-Five Point Questions

8. What was the denomination of the 1971 postal card issued as a tribute to America's hospitals?
9. The Great River Road was on a 1966 stamp. Where does it run?

Fifty-Point Question

10. In 1973 the U.S. issued a one-dollar coil using the same design as a sheet stamp issued in 1967. Who was the subject?

Quiz No. 40

Five-Point Questions

1. Who appears on the 1972 stamp honoring stamp collecting.
2. What sport is honored on a 1974 ten-cent commemorative?
3. Who is on the thirteen-cent stamp in the 1938 definitives?
4. The Great River Road is on a 1966 stamp. What river does the road follow?

Ten-Point Questions

5. What value is represented by the "C" stamps of 1981?
6. How many stamps make up each of the bicentennial souvenir sheets of 1976?
7. How many stamps are there in the butterfly issue of 1977?

Twenty-Five Point Questions

8. What law is honored on a 1964 postal card?
9. What is the denomination of the Parcel Post stamp of 1912 showing a letter carrier?

Fifty-Point Question

10. What Washington, D.C. building is shown on a 1947 ten-cent airmail stamp?

Colors

Quiz No. 41

Score 10 points for each correct answer.

1. What color would a stamp be if the Italian catalogue called it "Verde Mela?"
2. The French word "Noir" describes a stamp that is what color?
3. A stamp called "Azul" in Spanish would be what color?
4. What is the Italian word for brown?
5. A German catalog would call it "Weinrot." What color is it?
6. The Spanish word "Gris" describes what color stamp?
7. "Rouge, Rot and Rosso" all refer to what color stamp?
8. The German word "Gelb" describes what color stamp?
9. What would "flesh" colored stamps be called in French?
10. The German word "Zitronengelb" refers to what color stamp?

Countries

Quiz No. 42

You'll find the names of these countries on stamps. Tell where they are located and take 15 points for each correct answer.

1. Bahrain
2. Grenada
3. Burundi
4. Isle of Man
5. Angola
6. San Marino
7. Cape Verde
8. Bhutan
9. Dominica
10. Andorra

EUROPA

Quiz No. 43

Score 10 points for each correct answer.

1. What is the central design feature of the 1973 issue.
2. The 1971 issue uses three characteristics to describe the European Community. What are they?
3. What symbol appears on the 1968 issue?
4. In what year was the 10th anniversary of CEPT observed?
5. What was the design of the first EUROPA issue?
6. How many doves appear on the 1961-62 issue?
7. What flower appears on the 1964 issue?
8. In what year did "Leaves and Fruit" appear on EUROPA stamps?
9. How many countries issued EUROPA stamps in 1956?
10. What two industries are represented on the first issue?

First Day Covers

Quiz No. 44

Score 10 points for each correct answer.

1. What is the design called that is often found on the left hand side of a first day cover?
2. In what year did the U.S. first identify first day covers wih a distinctive cancellation?
3. What is the name given to covers using one or more stamps of different designs, not se-tenants?
4. What is the name of the collector group specializing in first day covers of the United States.
5. Who created the first modern first day cover by printing a cachet consisting of three lines of type on the Harding Memorial issue?
6. How can early first day covers be identified when they have no distinctive cancellation?
7. What U.S. stamp was the first to receive the "First Day of Issue" cancellation?
8. What options does a collector have in getting first day cancels through the U.S. Postal Service?
9. When a first day cover is damaged in the mail, what recourse does a collector have?
10. What is the rule if a stamp of a denomination less than the first class rate is submitted for first day cancellation?

Abbreviations

Quiz No. 45

Stamp collectors constantly run across abbreviations. Score ten points for each of these you can identify.

1. USPS
2. FDC
3. N.H.
4. O.G.
5. Perf.
6. CTO
7. Imperf.
8. Perfin.
9. Wmkd.
10. N.G.

Language

Quiz No. 46

Identify the following foreign words relating the stamp collecting. Score 15 points for each correct answer.

1. What does the German word "Flugpost" mean?
2. What is the Spanish word for cancellation?
3. What does the Italian word "Anullato" mean?
4. If a French stamp is described as showing "Armoiries," what does it show?
5. The German word "Markenrolle" describes what kind of stamp?
6. If you have a French stamp described as "faux" what kind of stamp do you have?
7. What is the German word for a definitive stamp?
8. A Spanish stamp described as "Sin dentar" would be what kind of stamp?
9. What is the Italian word for postmark?
10. What kind of stamps would the Germans call "Zeitungsmarke?"

Postmasters General

Quiz No. 47

Each of these men served as postmaster general of the United States. Identify the President under whom they served. Score 20 points for each correct answer.

1. Arthur E. Summerfield
2. Winton M. Blount
3. John Wanamaker
4. James A. Farley
5. J. Edward Day
6. Samuel Osgood
7. Albert S. Burleson
8. Lawrence O'Brien
9. Walter F. Brown
10. Robert E. Hannegan

Women on Stamps

Quiz No. 48

Five-Point Questions

1. What woman appears on the fifty-cent stamp of the 1954 Liberty Series?
2. The first woman Cabinet member in the U.S. appears on a 1980 commemorative. Who is she?
3. What is the profession of the four women shown on a 1952 three-cent stamp?
4. The founder of the American Red Cross appears on a 1948 stamp. Who is she?

Ten-Point Questions

5. What profession is honored on a four-cent issue of 1961?
6. The founder of the Girl Scouts appears on a 1948 stamp. Name her.
7. What First Lady appears on a miniature stamp issued in 1980?

Twenty-Five Point Questions

8. What nurse is honored on a thirteen-cent commemorative of 1976?
9. What 16-year-old girl appears on the "Contributors to the Cause" eight-cent issue of 1975?

Fifty-Point Question

10. A young woman appears on a tax stamp of 1935. What is the tax on?

General

Quiz No. 49

Score 10 points for each correct answer.

1. What does the word "Correos" mean on stamps of Spanish-speaking countries?
2. What are "se-tenant" stamps?
3. What are stamps called that are issued in rolls?
4. What are "cut squares?"
5. In what years did the U.S. issue "Grilled" stamps?
6. Stamps coated with phosphorescent material to enable mechanical sorting are called what kind of stamps?
7. What are stamps called when they are cancelled by the issuing government before they are sold at post offices?
8. What are "cinderellas?"
9. What does "bisect" mean to stamp collectors?
10. What is the term applied to impressions taken from an approved die, plate or stone in which the design and color are the same as the stamp issued to the public?

Quiz No. 50

Score 10 points for each correct answer.

1. What is the name applied to designs impressed into the paper on which stamps are printed?
2. When an overprint changes or restates the value of a stamp, what is it called?
3. What is a pair of stamps called when one stamp is upside down in relation to the other?
4. What company manufactured the piano that appears on the 8.4-cent bulk mail stamp?
5. What musical instrument appears on the U.S. 7.7-cent stamp?
6. What is the name given to the original engraved metal form from which plates are made for printing stamps?
7. What is the collector term for envelopes which have passed through the mail and bear postal markings?
8. In what year did the U.S. issue a five-cent stamp honoring American music?
9. What is the denomination of the Will Rogers stamp issued in 1979?
10. What musical instrument appears on the 3.1-cent stamp?

Quiz No. 51

Score 10 points for each correct answer.

1. Who is credited with being the first man to make an adhesive stamp?
2. What is the process called in which slits are cut between stamps to ease separation?
3. What is the device called which is used to measure the holes along the edges of a stamp?
4. What are APOs?
5. In what year did the twenty-four-cent airmail invert appear?
6. What is the name for an envelope stamp on which the color has inadvertently been omitted?
7. For what collector organization is APS the abbreviation?
8. For what collector group is SPA the abbreviation?
9. In what year did the U.S. experiment with the use of blue paper on its stamps?
10. In what U.S. stamp series is the "Broken Hat" issue a variety?

Quiz No. 52

Score 10 points for each correct answer.

1. What is the term used for stamps no longer valid for postage?
2. What are the impressions taken from a stamp die called?
3. In what part of stamp production is the "electric eye" used?
4. What are "fugitive colors?"
5. In what year did the U.S. first issue hunting stamps?
6. What does the term "Pro Juventute" found on the semi-postals of Switzerland mean?
7. What does the word "Spoorwegen" on Belgian parcel post stamps mean?
8. What company produced U.S. stamps from 1879 to 1894?
9. Selections of stamps from which you pick the ones you want and return the rest are called what?
10. What is the name given to a pattern pressed into a stamp paper to make it difficult to remove cancellation ink?

Australia

Quiz No. 53

Score 10 points for each correct answer.

1. The Parliament House of Australia is shown on a 1927 stamp. In what city is it?
2. What bird is shown on the 1929 issue marking the centenary of Western Australia?
3. What Australian animal is shown on the lowest value of the 1937-46 definitive set?
4. The visit of what royal couple in 1954 was the subject of a three-stamp set?
5. What youth group is honored on a 1948 stamp?
6. What opera singer is the subject of a 1961 commemorative?
7. The centenary of what organization is marked by a 1963 commemorative stamp?
8. What British hero appears on a 1965 commemorative?
9. What famous explorer is the subject of a 1970 set of stamps and a souvenir sheet?
10. Joseph B. Chifley is honored on a ten-cent stamp of 1975. What was his claim to fame?

Austria

Quiz No. 54

Score 10 points for each correct answer.

1. From 1867 to 1871 Austria and Hungary used the same stamps? Whose picture was on them?
2. What international language is the subject of a 1954 commemorative?
3. In 1959 Austria issued a stamp showing a large letter "E." What was it promoting?
4. Mercury and the Globe appear on a 1961 stamp. What convention did it publicize?
5. In what year did Austria issue a stamp marking the 125th anniversary of Austrian railroads?
6. What carnival ride is shown on the Prater Park 200th anniversary stamp of 1966?
7. Franz Grillparzer was honored on the centenary of his death in 1972. What was his claim to fame?
8. A map is featured on a 1972 commemorative. What industry does it honor?
9. Austrian police are shown on two means of transportation on a 1974 stamp. What are they?
10. A stamp collector is shown on a 1950 semi-postal. What is he doing?

Barbados

Quiz No. 55

Score 10 points for each correct answer.

1. Of what island group is Barbados a part?
2. What British hero is the subject of a 1966 set of four?
3. When did Barbados become independent?
4. A United Nations building appears on a 1968 stamp. In what city is it located?
5. Samuel Jackson Prescod appears on two 1971 stamps. What was his claim to fame?
6. What is the central design feature of the four-cent stamp marking the fifth anniversary of independence?
7. What kind of flowers are featured on the set of 18 issued between 1974 and 1977?
8. The Prudential Cup appears on a 1976 issue. In what sport is it awarded?
9. The victims of the eruption of what volcano benefitted from the 1979 semi-postals?
10. What, in addition to the denomination, is shown on the 1976 postage due stamps?

Belgium

Quiz No. 56

Score 10 points for each correct answer.

1. What two youth organizations are honored on a 1957 stamp?
2. Eugene Ysaye appears on a 1958 commemorative. Who was he?
3. The 500th anniversary of the birth of what Pope was marked by a 1959 set of two stamps?
4. A 1962 commemorative was issued in memory of concentration camp victims. What did it show?
5. What type airplane appears on the 1963 salute to Sabena Airlines?
6. A self-portrait of what Belgian painter appears on a 1966 stamp?
7. What is featured on the 1972 stamp marking the 50th anniversary of the economic union of Belgium and Luxembourg?
8. What king appears on a 1976 souvenir sheet?
9. What three Belgian kings appear on the 10-franc value of the 1915-20 definitives?
10. What three American astronauts are honored on a 1969 stamp?

Belize

Quiz No. 57

Score 10 points for each correct answer.

1. By what name was Belize formerly known?
2. What country lies immeditely to the north of Belize?
3. What animal is shown on the three-cent value of the Mayan pottery set of 1974?
4. What American is shown on the 1976 Bicentennial issue?
5. In what year did Belize become independent?
6. What vehicle is shown on the Churchill issue of 1974?
7. A "Crana" is shown on the lowest value of the 1974 definitive issue. What is it?
8. What distinguishes the designs of the postage due stamps of 1976 other than the numbers?
9. What group of people is shown with Queen Elizabeth II on the 1977 set honoring the 25th anniversary of her reign?
10. What is the occupation of the people shown on the lowest value of the 1975 Christmas issue?

Bermuda

Quiz No. 58

Score 10 points for each correct answer.

1. What queen is shown on the first general issue for Bermuda?
2. What is the top denomination of the 1910-1920 definitives?
3. What harbor is shown on the half-pence value of the 1936-40 definitives?
4. What stamp is shown on the 1949 set of three marking the centenary of Bermuda postage?
5. What sport is the subject of four stamps issued in 1973?
6. The silver cup and trophy awarded in what sport are shown on a 1976 set?
7. The Queen (Elizabeth II) visited Bermuda on her 25th anniversary as ruler. In what year did the visit occur?
8. What means of transportation is shown on six stamps issued in 1976?
9. Bermuda Girl Guides were honored on their anniversary in 1969. What anniversary was it?
10. The voyage of Sir George Somers is marked by four stamps issued in 1971. From where to where did he sail?

Canada

Quiz No. 59

Score 10 points for each correct answer.

1. A single stamp was issued in 1966 to promote public safety. What did it show?
2. In 1970 a Canadian Minister of Labor was kidnapped and killed. His picture is on a seven-cent stamp issued in 1971. Who was he?
3. The first bishop of Quebec was honored on the 350th anniversary of his birth on a 1973 stamp. Who was he?
4. In what year were the Olympic Games held in Montreal?
5. What American deputy postmaster general appears on a 1976 Canadian issue?
6. What bridge between the U.S. and Canada appears on a 1977 issue?
7. What birds are shown on the 1946 airmail stamps?
8. The use of what postal device is encouraged on a 1979 stamp?
9. In what year did Canada issue a set of provincial and territorial flags?
10. What topical subject dominated Canadian semi-postals?

Quiz No. 60

Score 10 points for each correct answer.

1. What ship appears on the fifty-cent definitive issue of 1928-29?
2. The 25th anniversary of the accession to the British throne of what ruler is marked by a 1935 set of stamps?
3. What two princesses appear on a 1939 issue marking a royal visit to Canada and the United States?
4. What kind of vessel is shown on the one-dollar definitive of the 1942-43 series?
5. The centenary of the birth of what inventor is marked by a 1947 commemorative?
6. The ship *Matthew* appears on a 1949 issue marking the entry of Newfoundland into confederation with Canada. To what explorer did it belong?
7. What fowl is shown flying over water on a 1952 seven-cent stamp?
8. What industry is honored with a two-stamp set issued in 1956?
9. What is shown on the Canadian stamp of 1957 honoring the Universal Postal Union?
10. Emily Pauline Johnson was the subject of a 1961 commemorative. What was her claim to fame?

Canal Zone

Quiz No. 61

Score 10 points for each correct answer.

1. When were the first Canal Zone stamps issued?
2. What explorer is shown on the one-cent Canal Zone stamp of 1906?
3. Who is shown on the three-cent stamp of 1934 marking the 20th anniversary of the opening of the Panama Canal?
4. What youth group is honored on the 1960 Canal Zone four-cent stamps?
5. Over what part of the Panama Canal is the plane flying in the 1931-1949 airmail set?
6. A seven-cent Canal Zone stamp of 1962 marks the fight against what disease?
7. How many postage due stamps were issued in the Canal Zone?
8. What explorer is honored on the overprinted postage due stamp of 1919?
9. What type aircraft is shown on four airmail stamps issued in 1939?
10. What ship is shown on the twelve and fifteen-cent stamps of 1917?

Central African Republic

Quiz No. 62

Score 10 points for each correct answer.

1. What sport is featured on the 1979 Olympic set?
2. Sir Rowland Hill, originator of Penny Postage, is shown on a 1979 stamp. What means of transportation also appears on the stamp?
3. What animal appears on the lowest value of the endangered animal series of 1978?
4. The coronation of what ruler is marked by a four-value set issued in 1977?
5. What book is the subject of a 1977 commemorative?
6. What rodents appear on a 1966 set?
7. What event is marked by a 1965 stamp showing a telegraph receiver?
8. What is the occupation of the woman shown on the International Negro Arts Festival stamp of 1966?
9. What device is shown on the 1963 stamp marking the 15th anniversary of the Universal Declaration of Human Rights?
10. What French leader is the subject of a 1971 commemorative?

Ceylon

Quiz No. 63

Score 10 points for each correct answer.

1. In what ocean is Ceylon located?
2. Who appears on the first stamps of Ceylon?
3. What industry is featured on the two-cent stamp in the set issued in 1938-1952?
4. What animal appears on the fifty-cent value of the same set?
5. What staple food appears on the 1966 issue?
6. On May 22, 1972, Ceylon changed its name. What is it now called?
7. D.S. Senanayake appears on a single stamp issued in 1966. What was his claim to fame?
8. The opening of an airport in what city was marked by a 1968 stamp?
9. The eradication of what disease was the subject of a 1962 issue?
10. A girl picking what crop is the subject of a 1-rupee issue of 1964-1969?

Chile

Quiz No. 64

Score 10 points for each correct answer.

1. What Pope is honored on a 1979 issue?
2. What vehicle is shown on the Red Cross commemorative of 1979?
3. What industry is the subject of a 1978 issue of two stamps?
4. What bird is shown on the Letter Writing Week Stamp of 1972?
5. A dove and a world map appear on a 1970 stamp. What organization does it honor?
6. The world championship of what sport held in Chile is honored on a 1966 stamp?
7. What Indian leader appears on a 1970 commemorative?
8. A block of four stamps issued in 1975 combines to form a single picture. What group does it honor?
9. What fruit is shown on the 1973 stamps promoting exports?
10. Chile's claim to what territory is shown on a 1947 set?

China

Quiz No. 65

Score 10 points for each correct answer.

1. What Chinese hero is the subject of the 1944-46 definitive set?
2. Whose picture is on the 1945 stamps marking the victory of the Allied Nations over Japan?
3. What American President appears on a 1959 stamp?
4. What sea creature appears on the 1961 stamp promoting mail order service?
5. What sport is saluted in the 1963 stamps marking the Asian Championship?
6. In 1968 four stamps were issued for the Olympics. What sport is shown on the lowest value?
7. What animals appear on the 1972 souvenir sheet?
8. What sport organization is honored on a 1973 set?
9. What animal appears on the 1974 New Year stamp?
10. In the Folk Tale stamp of 1975 a student is shown reading. What is the source of light?

Cook Islands

Quiz No. 66

Score 10 points for each correct answer.

1. How many islands make up the Cook Islands?
2. The "god" of what sport appears on a 1963 issue?
3. What sport appears on the fifteen-cent value of the set marking the Olympic Games in Mexico City?
4. What anniversary of Captain Cook's voyage of discovery is marked by a 1968 set?
5. What means of transportation is shown on 1973 set of seven stamps?
6. What member of the British Royal Family is shown on a twenty five-cent stamp issued in 1973?
7. What is the central design of the 1979 Christmas issue?
8. What space ship is the subject of a 1979 issue?
9. What use is made of the overprinted 1967-69 flower issue?
10. What shape are the 1969 stamps marking the South Pacific Games?

Czechoslovakia

Quiz No. 67

Score 10 points for each correct answer.

1. What fish appears on a 1955 stamps?
2. Views of what city are shown on a 1955 souvenir sheet?
3. What Peking building appears on a 1959 stamp?
4. How many stamps are shown on the 1960 issue for the Bratislava Stamp Exposition? (The 60h value).
5. What Soviet space ship is shown on a 1962 commemorative?
6. What animal appears on a set of six stamps in 1965?
7. What sport is featured on the lowest value of the 1972 Olympics set?
8. In what year were five stamps issued showing 18th century clocks?
9. Air post stamps of 1918-19 were surcharged in one of three different colors. What were they?
10. What U.S. airport is shown on a 1969 airmail stamp?

France

Quiz No. 68

Score 10 points for each correct answer.

1. What American appears on a 1976 French stamp?
2. What insect appears on a 1979 nature protection stamp?
3. What French leader appears on the 5-franc value of the 1863-70 definitive set?
4. What American President appears on the 1927 stamp honoring the visit of American Legionnaires to France in that year?
5. The self portrait of what artist appears on a stamp in the 1938-42 definitive set?
6. What two means of transportation are shown on the 1949 stamp publicizing Franco-American friendship?
7. What harbor, famous in World War II history, appears on a 1977 stamp?
8. What is the design of a semi-postal marking Stamp Day 1972?
9. A book and a globe are shown on an official stamp of 1966. What organization does it honor?
10. What aviation pioneer appears on a 1938 commemorative?

Germany

Quiz No. 69

Score 10 points for each correct answer.

1. The Confession of Augsburg appears on a 1980 stamp. Of what religious group is it the official creed?
2. What book is honored on a 1980 commemorative?
3. The 25th anniversary of Germany's membership in what organization is the subject of a 1980 stamp?
4. What famous author, a Nazi victim, appears on a 1979 stamp?
5. Gustav Stresemann, Ludwig Guidde and Carl von Ossietzky appear on a 1975 souvenir sheet. What is their claim to fame?
6. The world championships of what sport is marked by a 1975 stamp?
7. What German chancellor appears on a 1976 stamp?
8. What saint is the subject of a 1974 stamp?
9. What device invented by Wihelm Shickard appears on a 1973 stamp?
10. Germany's first poetess appears on a 1973 stamp. Who was she?

Quiz No. 70

Score 10 points for each correct answer.

1. An open book appears on a 1972 stamp. What does it mark?
2. What socialist leader appears on a 1970 stamp?
3. What Pope is the subject of a 1969 issue?
4. A 1969 souvenir sheet shows Marie Juchacz, Marie-Elizabeth Luders and Helen Weber. What does it honor?
5. A 1965 issue marks the 125th anniversary of postage stamps in Great Britain. From what countries are the illustrated stamps?
6. What U.S. President appears on a 1964 issue?
7. The re-election of what German President is marked by a 1964 stamp?
8. A 1961 stamp honors boy scouts of the world. Who is shown on the stamp?
9. What early automobile appears on a 1961 stamp?
10. What American statesman appears on a 1960 issue?

Ghana

Quiz No. 71

Score 10 points for each correct answer.

1. By what name was Ghana formerly known?
2. On what continent is Ghana located?
3. In what year did Ghana become independent?
4. What American monument appears on a 1959 issue?
5. What animal is shown on the one-pound issue of 1961?
6. What major change was marked by the issue of four stamps in 1965?
7. What historic event was saluted with a four-stamp set in 1970?
8. What aircraft appears on the flight anniversary issue of 1978?
9. What Christmas carol is featured on the eight-pence value of the 1979 Christmas set?
10. The introduction of what measuring system was marked by a 1975 issue?

Great Britain

Quiz No. 72

Score 10 points for each correct answer.

1. What member of the Royal Family is featured on a 1969 set?
2. The centenary of the birth of what Indian leader is marked by a 1969 commemorative?
3. What British author of "The Pickwick Papers" is honored on the centenary of his death in 1970?
4. What British stamp is reproduced on the 1970 issue for the London Philatelic Exhibition?
5. The wedding of what Royal couple is marked by a 1973 set?
6. The centenary of the birth of what British leader is marked by a 1974 set?
7. What type vessels are shown on a 1975 issue?
8. A 1975 set of five marked the sesquicentennial of public railroads in Great Britain. What railroad is represented on the seven-pence value?
9. The silver jubilee of what ruler is marked by a 1977 stamp set?
10. British wild flowers are shown on a 1979 set of four. Name any two of the flowers.

Quiz No. 73

Score 10 points for each correct answer.

1. What was the denomination of the first British stamps issued in 1840?
2. What Queen is shown on the first British set?
3. What was the color of the first British stamps?
4. What animal is shown on the stamp issued for the British Empire Exhibition in 1924?
5. What king is shown on the Peace issue of 1946?
6. What monarch is shown on the coronation issue of 1953?
7. What English writer was honored on a 1964 series?
8. Folk dancers from what country appear on a 1965 set?
9. The "Blood and Fire" flag appears on a 1965 issue. What organization does it honor?
10. What military aircraft is shown on the 1965 four-pence value?

Guernsey

Quiz No. 74

Score 10 points for each correct answer.

1. What form of government does Guernsey have?
2. In what body of water are the Guernsey Islands?
3. What famous printer is shown on a 1971 issue?
4. The stamp of what other British possession is shown on a 1971 Guernsey issue?
5. A 1972 issue marked the 25th wedding anniversary of Queen Elizabeth II. What does it show?
6. What animal is shown on a 1972 issue?
7. What British honor is Queen Elizabeth II shown wearing on a 1977 issue?
8. What building is shown on a 1979 issue?
9. The Town Church of St. Peter Port is shown on 12 stamps issued between 1977 and 1980. For what are they used?
10. What French writer who was a political exile in Guernsey is shown on a 1975 set?

Guyana

Quiz No. 75

Score 10 points for each correct answer.

1. What was the former name of Guyana?
2. On what continent is Guyana located?
3. In what year did Guyana gain its independence?
4. H.N. Critchlow appears on a 1979 set? The 60th anniversary of what organization does it honor?
5. A 1974 stamp carries the words: "One people, one nation, one destiny." What observance does it mark?
6. What Indian leader is shown on a 1969 set?
7. What common prayer is shown on the 1971 Christmas stamp?
8. The stamp of what country is shown on the Universal Postal Union issue of 1974?
9. The independence of what country is marked by a 1975 set?
10. A 1977 set shows coins. What does it mark?

Hong Kong

Quiz No. 76

Score 10 points for each correct answer.

1. What is the political status of Hong Kong?
2. At the mouth of what river is Hong Kong located?
3. What Queen is shown on the first Hong Kong issue?
4. What animal is shown on the stamps for the Lunar Year 1973?
5. What is the design of Hong Kong postage due stamps?
6. What kind of dog is shown on the 1970 Lunar Year stamps?
7. What tunnel links Victoria and Kowloon? It appears on a 1972 stamp.
8. What king appears on the regular issues of 1912-14?
9. The statue of what queen appears on the 1962 stamps marking the centenary of Hong Kong stamps?
10. What bird is shown on the stamp marking the centenary of the Universal Postal Union?

Hungary

Quiz No. 77

Score 10 points for each correct answer.

1. What group of buildings is shown on a 1964 series?
2. What American first lady appears on a 1964 issue?
3. A child with a towel and a toothbrush is shown on a 1963 issue. What organization does it honor?
4. What sport is shown on a 1962 souvenir sheet?
5. What flower is shown on the 1959 Labor Day issue?
6. What occupation is the subject of 1956 stamp?
7. How many stamps are there in the 1966 issue for the European Athletic Championships?
8. What space ship appears on the 5-forint stamp issued in 1967?
9. What lyric poet is the subject of a 1969 commemorative?
10. The "Portrait of a Man" is shown on a 1971 stamp marking the 500th anniversary of the birth of the painter. Who was he?

India

Quiz No. 78

Score 10 points for each correct answer.

1. What Queen was shown on the first stamps of India?
2. By what trading company were the first stamps of India produced?
3. What animals are shown on the 1951 stamp marking the centenary of the founding of the Geological Survey of India?
4. What flower is shown on the 1954 stamp issued for United Nations Day?
5. What U.S. made plane is shown on the 1961 stamp honoring the 50th aniversary of the world's first air mail?
6. What Indian prime minister appears on a 1964 commemorative?
7. The hand of what religious leader is shown on a 1972 commemorative?
8. What occupation is featured on the stamp issued for the 1977 philatelic exhibition?
9. What aircraft is shown on the 1948 air mail stamp?
10. What bird appears on the 1979 stamp honoring the International Atomic Energy Conference?

Ireland

Quiz No. 79

Score 10 points for each correct answer.

1. What poet appears on a 1952 commemorative?
2. What saint is featured on the Holy Year Stamp of 1950?
3. What musical instrument is on the 1952 stamp honoring the poet Thomas Moore?
4. What building appears on the 1964 stamps issued to honor the New York World's Fair?
5. What is the central design feature of the 1968 EUROPA stamps?
6. What religious leader appears on a 1979 commemorative?
7. The founder of the Sisters of Mercy is honored on a 1978 stamp. Who is she?
8. What youth group is honored on a 1977 set of two stamps?
9. Maple leaves appear on a 1967 stamp. What was the occasion?
10. Birds appear on a set of four stamps issued in 1979. Name two of the four birds.

Israel

Quiz No. 80

Score 10 points for each correct answer.

1. What American President appears on a 1975 stamp?
2. The founder of Zionism was the subject of a 1978 issue. Who was he?
3. The first President of Israel appears on a stamp in the same set. Who was he?
4. What body of water is shown on a 1952 airmail stamp?
5. What animal appears on the postage due stamps of 1952?
6. What craft is the subject of a 1963 stamp?
7. Israel's President from 1952 to 1963 appears on a 1964 stamp. Who was he?
8. What are the youngsters doing on the 1958 stamp for the First World Conference of Jewish Youth?
9. The 50th anniversary of what city is marked on a 1959 issue?
10. What vehicle is shown on the 1955 Red Cross issue?

Italy

Quiz No. 81

Score 10 points for each correct answer.

1. What physicist appears on a 1979 issue?
2. In what year did Italy issue two stamps for the World Bicycling Championship?
3. What opera house is the subject of a 1978 issue?
4. What sport is shown on the 1977 Stamp Day issue?
5. The 400th anniversary of the death of what Venetian painter is marked by a 1976 issue?
6. A 1973 stamp shows a map of Italy and the emblem of a service group. What is the group?
7. What anniversary of the birth of Michelangelo de Caravaggio is marked by a 1973 issue?
8. What world-famous tourist attraction appears on a 1973 stamp?
9. Saverio Mercadante is honored on a 1970 stamp. What was his occupation?
10. What patriot is the subject of a 1955 air mail stamp?

Jamaica

Quiz No. 82

Score 10 points for each correct answer.

1. In what body of water is Jamaica located?
2. What ruler is shown on the 1952 Boy Scout issue?
3. In what year did Jamaica gain independence?
4. What British leader appears on a 1966 set?
5. The Jamaica Pavilion at what exposition is featured on a 1967 stamp?
6. Sir Alexander and Lady Bustamente appear on a 1968 set. What does it mark?
7. The introduction of what animal to Jamaica is marked by a 1973 set?
8. What instrument is being played on the lowest value of the 1977 set honoring the Jamaica Military Band?
9. What scientific venture is saluted by a three-cent stamp set issued in 1972?
10. What is the central design feature of the 1976 set marking the 21st Olympic Games?

Japan

Quiz No. 83

Score 10 points for each correct answer.

1. What is the central feature of the design of the 1952 airmail stamps?
2. In what year did the first airmail stamps of Japan appear?
3. Japan issued a semi-postal souvenir sheet in 1948. What two organizations did it benefit?
4. A 1979 stamp shows a boy floating in space. What event did it commemorate?
5. What sport is the subject of a 1979 stamp?
6. What prehistoric animal is shown on the 1977 stamp for the centenary of the National Science Museum?
7. What vehicle is shown on the 1976 stamp marking the 50th anniversary of Hirohito's accession to the throne?
8. What sport is featured on the 1969 stamp for the National Athletic meet?
9. A girl bouncing a ball is on a 1957 stamp. What is the occasion?
10. What national park is the subject of a 1953 issue?

Korea

Quiz No. 84

Score 10 points for each correct answer.

1. What American general appears on a 1965 stamp?
2. In what year were the first Korean stamps issued?
3. What bird appears on the 1964 stamp marking the first anniversary of liberation?
4. Korea's first president appears on a 1948 stamp. Who was he?
5. What method of transportation is the subject of a 1949 stamp?
6. What is the central design feature of the lowest value of the 1957 Christmas set?
7. What flower is shown on the 1960 issue marking the inaugural session of the House of Councilors?
8. What youth group is featured on a 1961 stamp?
9. What two countries are honored on the 1965 stamp of the Korean Military Assistance Group?
10. Korea's first General Postmaster is shown on a 1964 stamp for the 80th anniversary of the Korean Postal System. Who is he?

Lesotho

Quiz No. 85

Score 10 points for each correct answer.

1. What was the former name of Lesotho?
2. On what continent is Lesotho located?
3. A triangular stamp issued in 1967 shows the statue of what king?
4. What Boy Scout leader appears on a 1967 issue?
5. What industry is shown on the lowest value of an occupation set issued in 1971?
6. The International Year of the Child was marked by a 1979 set. What is shown on the lowest value?
7. What University was honored on a 1974 four-stamp set?
8. A man with a cane is shown on a 1977 set. What does it mark?
9. The Wright Brothers' airplane appears on a 1978 set. What does the set honor?
10. Ndlamo, Baleseli and Hohobelo are the subjects of a 1975 set. What are they?

Liberia

Quiz No. 86

Score 10 points for each correct answer.

1. The first president of Liberia is shown on a 1961 airmail stamp. Who was he?
2. That map of what continent is shown on a 1960 airmail?
3. The 75th birthday of what Liberian President was marked by a 1970 commemorative?
4. What two U.S. Presidents appear on 1964 issues?
5. What U.N. Secretary-General appears on a 1962 issue?
6. What sport is the subject of a six-cent value in the 1956 Olympics set?
7. What is the shape of the animal stamps of 1937?
8. What monument appears on the 1956 three-cent stamp honoring FIPEX?
9. What American Black leader appears on a 1968 stamp?
10. The Royal Family of what country appears on a 1971 airmail souvenir sheet?

Luxembourg

Quiz No. 87

Score 10 points for each correct answer.

1. What Roman coin appears on the 5-franc value of the coin stamps of 1979?
2. What sport is the subject of a single 1972 stamp?
3. What bird appears on the lowest value of the animal protection set of 1961?
4. What kind of fish is shown on the 1963 stamp for the World Fly-Fishing Championship?
5. In what year were stamps first issued in Luxembourg?
6. What is the subject of the 1975 semi-postal set?
7. What river is shown on the one-franc airmail stamp of 1946?
8. What is shown on the watermark of the 1928 official stamps?
9. What British hero appears on a 1974 stamp?
10. What kind of stamps are covered by Scott listing NB1-NB9?

Mexico

Quiz No. 88

Score 10 points for each correct answer.

1. What revolutionary leader appears on a 1978 airmail?
2. A dancer from what Indian group appears on the 1.60-peso issue of 1977?
3. What explorer is the subject of the 1967 airmail stamp for International Tourist Year?
4. The visit of what U.S. president is marked by a 1962 issue?
5. What volcano appears on a 1956 airmail issue?
6. What is shown on the 1971 stamp honoring composer Augustin Lara?
7. What stamp is shown on the 1940 issue marking the centenary of the postage stamp?
8. The visit of what U.N. Secretary General was marked by a 1966 airmail issue?
9. The 200th anniversary of the birth of what composer was the subject of a 1970 stamp?
10. What is the central design feature of the 1972 airmail marking the 74th assembly of the International Tourist Alliance?

Monaco

Quiz No. 89

Score 10 points for each correct answer.

1. What is the shape of the 10-centime stamp in the Franklin D. Roosevelt series of 1946?
2. In what year were stamps issued marking the enthronement of Prince Ranier III?
3. What medical missionary is honored on a commemorative issued in 1955?
4. What American president appears on a 1956 stamp?
5. In what year were Princess Grace and Prince Rainier married?
6. Two Popes are shown on a 1958 issue. Who are they?
7. What American car maker appears on a 1963 issue?
8. What two American presidents appear on a 1970 stamp?
9. What breed of dog is shown on the 1976 issue for the International Dog Show?
10. The stamps of three countries appear on the 1960 issue honoring the 60th anniversary of Monaco stamps. Name the countries.

Netherlands

Quiz No. 90

Score 10 points for each correct answer.

1. What king appears on the first Netherlands stamps?
2. What lady became Queen of the Netherlands at age 18?
3. What occupation is shown on a ten-cent 1952 stamp?
4. The silver anniversary of what rulers was marked by two stamps in 1962?
5. What sport is the subject of a 1974 stamp?
6. Three countries are honored on the "BENELUX" isssue of 1974. What are they?
7. Martinus Nijhoff was honored on a 1954 semi-postal. What was his claim to fame?
8. What painter created "The Laughing Child" that appears on a 1937 semi-postal?
9. What is the profession of the three men shown on a set of three stamps issued in 1980?
10. Postage due stamps of the Netherlands also were used in three others areas in different colors. What are the areas?

Nicaragua

Quiz No. 91

Score 10 points for each correct answer.

1. In what year were the first stamps of Nicaragua issued?
2. What building is shown on the 1930 series of 11 stamps?
3. What famous philatelic pioneer is the subject of a 1950 issue?
4. What American clergyman appears on a 1959 stamp?
5. What soccer star appears on a 1970 issue?
6. The re-election of what president is marked by a 1975 set?
7. What means of transportation is shown on the two-cent stamp of 1978 honoring powered flight?
8. A Goya painting of what saint appears on the 1978 Christmas stamp?
9. What two American astronauts appear on a 1967 stamp?
10. The presidents of Mexico and Nicaragua are shown on a 1968 stamp. Name them.

Norway

Quiz No. 92

Score 10 points for each correct answer.

1. What flowers are shown on a 1977 set of two stamps?
2. What is the central design of the 1969 census stamps?
3. What means of transportation is shown on a 1963 set?
4. Henri Dunant is shown on a 1961 issue. What was his claim to fame?
5. What explorer of the South Pole is honored on a 1961 set?
6. What king is shown on the regular issue of 1958-1960?
7. What institute of learning is the subject of a 1961 set?
8. The centenary of the birth of what composer is the subject of the 1943 set of four stamps?
9. A 1965 semi-postal set shows a severed chain and a dove. What does it celebrate?
10. The centenary of the birth of what king was observed by a 1972 stamp issue?

Philippines

Quiz No. 93

Score 10 points for each correct answer.

1. In what year did the Philippines become independent?
2. How did Jose Rizal die?
3. What Philippine president is shown on a 1947 souvenir sheet?
4. What American president appears on a 1960 stamp?
5. What Mexican president is shown on a 1963 stamp?
6. In what year did Ferdinand E. Marcos become president of the Philippines?
7. The 25th anniversary of the landing of U.S. forces on what Philippine Island was marked by a stamp set in 1969?
8. What aircraft appears on the 1977 stamp marking the 50th anniversary of airmail service from Key West to Havana?
9. What animal is shown on a 1977 airmail marking a philatelic exhibition?
10. What means of transportation appears on the 1947 special delivery stamp?

Poland

Quiz No. 94

Score 10 points for each correct answer.

1. The 25th anniversary of the signing of what treaty was marked by a stamp issued in 1980?
2. The originator of penny postage was the subject of a 1979 stamp. Who was he?
3. What American President appears on a 1975 stamp?
4. In 1975 four stamps appeared showing cartoon characters. What were they saluting?
5. What animals appear on a 50-groszy stamp of 1975?
6. What Polish composer is the subject of a 1970 stamp?
7. What bird is the national symbol of Poland?
8. What Polish patriot, a general in the American Revolution, appears on a 1967 set?
9. What American First Lady appears on a 1964 stamp?
10. What kind of boats are racing for the European championships on the low value of the 1961 set?

San Marino

Quiz No. 95

Score 10 points for each correct answer.

1. Within what country is San Marino located?
2. What explorer is the subject of a 1952 issue?
3. What American President appears on a 1959 issue?
4. What pioneer auto maker appears on the one-lira value of the 1962 auto set?
5. The 700th anniversary of the birth of what poet is honored on a 1965 set?
6. What American movie maker appears on a 1970 set?
7. What aviation pioneers are commemorated on a 1978 airmail set?
8. What organization is the subject of a semi-postal special delivery stamp of 1923?
9. What type plane appears on the 1974 airmail set?
10. The founder of Lions International appears on a 1960 stamp. Who was he?

Spain

Quiz No. 96

Score 10 points for each correct answer.

1. What sport is the subject of a 1980 set of two stamps?
2. The coats of arms and kings of what country are shown on a 1979 set?
3. What South American liberators appear on a 1978 set?
4. What American inventor is honored on a 1976 stamp?
5. The works of what type craftsmen are shown on a 1975 set?
6. What animal is shown on the issue for International Stamp Day in 1965?
7. What Pope is shown on a 1962 issue?
8. El Greco's painting of what saint appears on a 1961 stamp?
9. By what other name was Charles V known? He appears on a 1958 set.
10. What was the purpose of the Franchise Stamps of 1869?

Sweden

Quiz No. 97

Score 10 points for each correct answer.

1. What type fish are shown on the 1979 stamp honoring sea research?
2. What king is shown on a 1962 series of semi-postals?
3. What city is the plane flying over on the 1930 airmail stamps?
4. What festive day is featured on the EUROPA isssue of 1975?
5. What is shown on the first two Swedish stamps?
6. What saint is featured on a 1941 stamp?
7. Hjalmar Branting is shown on a 1960 stamp. What was his position in the Swedish government?
8. What sport is featured on a 1967 issue?
9. What ancient warship, salvaged in 1961, is shown on a 1969 set?
10. What famous singer appears on the 1975 stamp for International Women's Year?

Switzerland

Quiz No. 98

Score 10 points for each correct answer.

1. A souvenir sheet was issued in 1974 for the centenary of the Universal Postal Union. What did it show?
2. What Swiss military unit is honored on a 1965 stamp?
3. Two 1843 stamps are shown on a 1968 issue. From what cities do they come?
4. What type of transportation is shown on a four-stamp issue of 1947?
5. What is the central design feature of the National Defense semi-postals of 1936?
6. A 1980 semi-postal series shows trade and craft signs. What business does the "40 + 20" value stamp show?
7. What weed appears on a 1960 semi-postal?
8. The "Ville de Lucerne" appears on a 1975 stamp. What is it?
9. A souvenir sheet of four stamps was issued September 29, 1934. What did it honor?
10. Alexandre Yersin appears on a 1971 stamp. What was his occupation?

United Nations

Quiz No. 99

Score 10 points for each correct answer.

1. In what year were the first United Nations stamps issued?
2. What was the highest value of the first U.N. definitive set?
3. What did the 1954 stamp honoring the Food and Agricultural Organization show?
4. U.N. commemoratives of 1956 were issued in two denominations. What were they?
5. What U.N. organization is featured on the commemoratives of 1956?
6. What is the design of the 1961 issue for the International Court of Justice?
7. Three stamps were issued in 1964 saluting education for progress. What was the common design?
8. What building is shown on the twenty-cent definitive of the 1965- 66 series?
9. Who designed the stained glass window shown on the 1967 souvenir sheet?
10. Who designed the statue shown on the seventy-five-cent stamp in the Art at the U.N. Series of 1968?

Vatican City

Quiz No. 100

Score 10 points for each correct answer.

1. In what year were the first Vatican stamps issued?
2. What Pope appears on a 1933 issue?
3. The Bicentenary of the death of what saint is marked by a 1975 set?
4. A painting by Fra Angelico appears on the International-al Women's Year set of 1975. What does it show?
5. The first Vatican semi-postals were issued to mark a Holy Year. What year was it?
6. The statue of what saint appears on the first Vatican airmail?
7. What does the word "Segnatasse" mean on Vatican stamps?
8. Father Angelo Secchi appears on a 1979 stamp. What was his profession?
9. How many semi-postal stamps did the Vatican issue between 1933 and 1980?
10. What is the central design feature of the postage due stamps of 1968?

Answers

Quiz No. 1

1. Columbia University in New York City
2. Five Cents
3. The Frigate Constitution
4. Pocahontas
5. Golf
6. Diamond Head, Honolulu, Hawaii
7. All printed by private firms
8. Zachary Taylor
9. 1900
10. Daniel Chester French

Quiz No. 2

1. Twenty-four cents
2. Amelia Earhart and Blanche Stuart Scott
3. John F. Kennedy
4. Daniel Boone
5. 1938
6. Dental Health
7. Fort Dearborn
8. 1939
9. Green
10. Hereford Steer

Quiz No. 3

1. Four
2. Detroit, Michigan
3. Three cents
4. Purple
5. Calvin Coolidge
6. Auto racing
7. Ten cents
8. Queen Isabella and Columbus
9. Physical fitness
10. The Great Seal of the United States

Quiz No. 4

1. Six cents
2. Charles Lindbergh
3. Liberty
4. Four
5. Ten cents
6. Women Marines
7. Deep orange
8. William McKinley
9. 1853
10. A kerosene table lamp

Quiz No. 5

1. W.C. Fields
2. Four and eight cents
3. Dutch
4. Eight
5. Two cents
6. The Charter Oak
7. Baseball
8. Gerard Davis
9. 1970
10. Eugene O'Neill

Quiz No. 6

1. Quilt making
2. Skiing
3. Soyuz
4. Whooping cranes
5. Five
6. One, three, four and four cents
7. Jane Addams
8. China Clipper
9. 1959
10. Alexander Hamilton

Quiz No. 7

1. George Washington
2. George Washington
3. San Francisco
4. Winston Churchill
5. Dr. Crawford W. Long
6. Gymnast
7. John Marshall
8. 90 cents
9. D.W. Griffith
10. Postal clerk

Quiz No. 8

1. Thomas Jefferson
2. Tom Sawyer
3. Six
4. Robert H. Goddard
5. Nicolaus Copernicus
6. Green
7. John James Audubon
8. Basketball
9. Eagle
10. 1907

Quiz No. 9

1. America's Cup
2. Thirteen
3. John Tyler
4. One-cent
5. Arch of Triumph, Paris
6. 1940
7. Camellia
8. Rose carmine
9. Warren G. Harding
10. 1915

Quiz No. 10

1. Ten
2. One-cent
3. John Quincy Adams
4. Will Rogers
5. Five cents
6. 1945
7. William McKinley
8. Books, bookmark, eyeglasses
9. Montgomery Blair, 1963
10. July 1, 1851

Quiz No. 11

1. Hungary
2. Eighteen
3. Theodore Roosevelt
4. Danish West Indies
5. Three cents
6. 1,000th
7. 1948
8. James Fenimore Cooper
9. Adlai Stevenson
10. Robert E. Lee, Jefferson Davis and Stonewall Jackson

Quiz No. 12

1. Two cents
2. Yes
3. Four
4. Woodrow Wilson
5. Magnolia
6. Samuel L. Clemens
7. 1931
8. Red violet
9. 1939
10. Columbia Jays

Quiz No. 13

1. Dictionaries
2. James Monroe
3. Dr. Walter Reed
4. Two
5. Elizabeth Clarke Copley, daughter of John Copley
6. 1940
7. Five cents
8. Four
9. One dollar
10. Virginia of Sagadohock

Quiz No. 14

1. July 4, 1946
2. Andrew Jackson
3. Five cents
4. John F. Kennedy
5. Columbus
6. 1972
7. San Juan, Puerto Rico
8. Ultramarine
9. Locomotive, tricycle, horse and baby carriage
10. Savannah

Quiz No. 15

1. Bicycle
2. Poland
3. James K. Polk
4. Four
5. 1959
6. George Gershwin
7. Holding a medal
8. Zion Park, Utah
9. Giant Saguaro Cactus
10. Cardinal and Brown Pelican

Quiz No. 16

1. Booker T. Washington
2. Patrick Henry
3. Lake Placid, New York
4. Triangle
5. 19th, Women's Suffrage
6. Ten cents
7. 1959
8. Rutherford B. Hayes
9. Niagara Falls
10. A railroad conductor's lantern

Quiz No. 17

1. Four
2. Ohio River
3. Sunflower
4. Basketball
5. The White House
6. William Allen White
7. Alfred E. Smith
8. Korea (KORPA)
9. Louisa May Alcott
10. Capt. William O. Bucky O'Neill

Quiz No. 18

1. Ramon Magsaysay of the Philippines
2. Samuel F.B. Morse
3. City Mail Delivery
4. Fifty
5. Five cents
6. Peace Corps
7. Fort Harrod
8. The Sloop Restaurationen
9. Peter Stuyvesant in 1948 issue
10. One is perf 11, one 11 x 10 1/2 and one a horizontal coil.

Quiz No. 19

1. Win the War
2. Battle of White Plains
3. John Adams
4. New York Times
5. Two
6. New Jersey
7. Eight
8. Seamstress
9. Airplane
10. William H. Seward

Quiz No. 20

1. Quakers
2. Martha Washington
3. Martha Washington
4. Tadeusz Kosciuszko
5. Four Cents
6. W.C. Handy
7. Cancer
8. Dark brown
9. Freedom of Speech and Religion, from War and from Fear
10. Abraham Lincoln

Quiz No. 21

1. Harry Truman
2. George Eastman
3. Mount McKinley
4. Theodore Roosevelt
5. Franklin Pierce
6. 1847
7. 1931
8. Dark brown
9. Ulysses S. Grant
10. Benjamin Franklin

Quiz No. 22

1. Ship building
2. May 1, 1977
3. Yellowstone
4. Buffalo
5. Zachary Taylor
6. Sprinting
7. 65¢, $1.30 and $2.60
8. Ralph Waldo Emerson
9. Iron Betty
10. Motorcycle

Quiz No. 23

1. National Parks
2. Herbert Hoover
3. Pennsylvania
4. Secretary of State 1933-44
5. Minnesota
6. James A. Garfield
7. One and one-quarter cents
8. Train
9. Blue green
10. Cities, Parks, Street and Highways

Quiz No. 24

1. Camellia
2. Martin Van Buren
3. One dollar
4. Benjamin Franklin
5. Tennis
6. A coach
7. William Howard Taft
8. 1936
9. Bright red violet
10. 1862 by John Gault of Boston

Quiz No. 25

1. San Francisco Bay
2. Abraham Lincoln
3. One cent
4. Abraham Lincoln
5. Robert A. Taft
6. Triangle
7. Palace of Governors, Santa Fe, New Mexico
8. "The Wake of the Ferry"
9. Twenty-four cents
10. 1845

Quiz No. 26

1. 300th
2. Four
3. Magnolia
4. New York
5. Andrew Johnson
6. Her parents
7. 1940
8. AFL-CIO
9. Moby Dick, the whale
10. Luther Burbank

Quiz No. 27

1. Fifteen cents
2. Seattle, Washington
3. San Antonio, Texas
4. Moina Michael
5. Globe and Wing
6. U.S. Coast Guard Cutter Eagle
7. 7.9 cents
8. Aircraft carrier
9. George and Martha Washington
10. May 20, 1902

Quiz No. 28

1. Sagamore Hill
2. Dog
3. Five cents
4. The Old Man of the Mountain
5. San Antonio, Texas
6. S.S. Dorchester
7. Grover Cleveland
8. A track runner and a discus thrower
9. Sepia and yellow
10. Robert R. Livingston

Quiz No. 29

1. The Dove of Peace
2. Red violet
3. Czechoslovakia
4. Four cents
5. Eight
6. Quill pen
7. 49
8. James A. Garfield
9. 16
10. "New Netherland"

Quiz No. 30

1. The Headless Horseman
2. Abraham Lincoln
3. Benjamin Franklin
4. Red rose
5. Horace Greeley
6. 1948
7. Two cents
8. Wild turkey, pronghorn antelope and king salmon
9. Balboa
10. Decatur House

Quiz No. 31

1. Six cents
2. The Philippines
3. Mail order
4. Washington Irving
5. Providence, Rhode Island
6. Swinging a bat
7. Poet
8. Troops guarding a wagon train
9. Angus and Longhorn
10. General Francis Marion

Quiz No. 32

1. Piano
2. Neil Armstrong
3. The Netherlands
4. Italy
5. New York and Washington
6. New Jersey
7. Winslow Homer
8. The Pan American Exposition Series
9. Chester A. Arthur
10. Wolf Trap Farm in Virginia

Quiz No. 33

1. Washington, D.C.
2. Jefferson Davis
3. Ski jumping
4. 100th
5. Brussels, Belgium
6. 1962
7. Alexandria, Virginia
8. Centenary of the opening of the Soo Locks
9. Canal Zone seal
10. Thomas Hart Benton

Quiz No. 34

1. 1982
2. Finland
3. Alaska
4. Baseball and football
5. Frederic Remington
6. Four
7. Six cents
8. 1815
9. Chief Justice of the U.S.
10. Roanoke Island

Quiz No. 35

1. Independence Hall
2. John Philip Sousa
3. Mexico
4. The Bible
5. Tennis
6. Two
7. Four cents
8. The Legend of Sleepy Hollow
9. Black
10. S.S. Adriatic

Quiz No. 36

1. Emily Dickinson
2. Fifty
3. James Madison
4. Venezuela
5. Cordell Hull, 1933-44
6. Knoxville, Tennessee
7. The Philippines
8. 11 cents
9. Poet
10. Fredericksburg, Virginia

Quiz No. 37

1. Arizona
2. Six cents
3. 100th
4. James Buchanan
5. U.S. and Canada
6. Thomas Jefferson
7. All U.S. cities
8. Washington, D.C
9. The Homestead Act
10. 1873

Quiz No. 38

1. Locomotive
2. James A. Naismith
3. No
4. William Henry Harrison
5. Four cents
6. Fulton, Missouri
7. Four
8. Princeton University
9. Five cents
10. Chicago, Illinois

Quiz No. 39

1. Casey Jones
2. India
3. Carmine
4. 1975
5. Benjamin Franklin
6. Santa Maria
7. Hawaii
8. Six cents
9. New Orleans to Ontario, Canada
10. Eugene O'Neill

Quiz No. 40

1. Benjamin Franklin
2. Horse racing
3. Millard Fillmore
4. Mississippi
5. Twenty cents
6. Five
7. Four
8. Social Security Act
9. Two cents
10. Pan American Building

Quiz No. 41

1. Apple Green
2. Black
3. Blue
4. Bruno
5. Claret
6. Gray
7. Red
8. Yellow
9. Chair
10. Citron

Quiz No. 42

1. Persian Gulf near Saudi Arabia
2. Southernmost of the West Indies
3. Central Africa, with Rwanda on the North and Zaire on the West
4. In the Irish Sea 20 miles from Scotland
5. On the Atlantic Coast of Southwest Africa
6. North Central Italy near the Adriatic Coast
7. In the Atlantic Ocean off the Western tip of Africa
8. In the Eastern Himalayas Mountains with India on the West and South and China on the North
9. Eastern Caribbean with Guadeloupe to the North and Martinique to the South
10. In the Pyrenees Mountains with Spain on the South and France on the North

Quiz No. 43

1. Post Horn and Arrows
2. Fraternity, Cooperation and Common Effort
3. Golden Key
4. 1969
5. "E" and Dove
6. Nineteen
7. Daisy
8. 1965
9. Six
10. Coal and Steel

Quiz No. 44

1. Cachet
2. 1937
3. Combination Covers
4. American First Day Cover Society
5. George W. Linn
6. The date
7. The Northwest Territory Ordinance Issue of 1937
8. Either buying and affixing the stamps themselves or sending payment to the postmaster in the issue city
9. Immediate return to the postmaster in the first day city for replacement
10. Postage must be added to bring it up to the first class rate

Quiz No. 45

1. United States Postal Service
2. First Day Cover
3. Never Hinged
4. Original Gum
5. Perforated
6. Cancelled to Order
7. Imperforate
8. Perforated Initials
9. Watermarked
10. No Gum

Quiz No. 46

1. Airmail
2. Matasello
3. Cancelled
4. Coats of Arms
5. Coil
6. Counterfeit
7. Freimarken
8. Imperforate
9. Bollo
10. Newspaper Stamps

Quiz No. 47

1. Dwight D. Eisenhower, 1953
2. Richard N. Nixon, 1969
3. William H. Harrison, 1889
4. Franklin D. Roosevelt, 1933
5. John F. Kennedy, 1961
6. George Washington, 1789
7. Woodrow Wilson, 1913
8. Lyndon B. Johnson, 1965
9. Herbert Hoover, 1929
10. Harry S Truman, 1945

Quiz No. 48

1. Susan B. Anthony
2. Frances Perkins
3. Armed Forces
4. Clara Barton
5. Nursing
6. Juliette Gordon Low
7. Dolley Madison
8. Clara Maass
9. Sybil Ludington
10. Potatoes

Quiz No. 49

1. Postage
2. Stamps joined together in an unsevered pair, strip or block differing in design, denomination or overprint
3. Coils
4. Cuttings from a postal stationery (usually stamped envelopes) leaving a border around the stamp
5. 1867-1870
6. Tagged
7. Precancels
8. Seals, local revenues, labels, poster stamps and similar "non-postage" material
9. A stamp usually cut in half for use in emergency situations
10. Proof

Quiz No. 50

1. Watermark
2. Surcharge
3. Tete-Beche
4. Steinway in 1857
5. Saxhorns
6. Die
7. Covers
8. 1964
9. Fifteen cents
10. Guitar

Quiz No. 5I

1. Sir Rowland Hill
2. Rouletting
3. Perforation Gauge
4. Army Post Office
5. 1918
6. Albino
7. American Philatelic Society
8. Society of Philatelic Americans
9. 1908
10. 1893 Columbian Series

Quiz No. 52

1. Demonetized
2. Die Proofs
3. Perforation
4. Colors that run when wet
5. 1934
6. For Youth
7. Railroad
8. American Bank Note Company
9. Approvals
10. Grill

Quiz No. 53

1. Canberra
2. Black Swan
3. Kangaroo
4. Queen Elizabeth II and the Duke of Edinburgh
5. Boy Scouts
6. Dame Nellie Melba
7. International Red Cross
8. Winston Churchill
9. Captain James Cook
10. Prime Minister. He lived from 1885 to 1951

Quiz No. 54

1. Emperor Franz Josef
2. Esperanto
3. European Unity
4. The International Banking Congress
5. 1962
6. Ferris Wheel
7. Dramatic poet
8. Austrian Telephone System
9. Horse and Motorcycle
10. Examining a cover with a magnifying glass

Quiz No. 55

1. West Indies
2. Winston Churchill
3. November 10, 1966
4. Santiago, Chile
5. First Black member of the Barbados Assembly
6. Coat of Arms
7. Orchids
8. Cricket
9. Mount Soufriere
10. Flowers

Quiz No. 56

1. Boy and Girl Scouts
2. Violinist and Composer
3. Adrian VI
4. Two hands, one enclosed in barbed wire
5. Caravelle
6. Rik Wouters
7. Coins
8. Baudouin
9. Leopold I, Albert I, Leopold II
10. Armstrong, Collins and Aldrin

Quiz No. 57

1. British Honduras
2. Mexico
3. Stag
4. William Wrigley, Jr.
5. 1973
6. Coronation Coach of Elizabeth II
7. A fish
8. Each has a different border
9. Bishops
10. Musicians

Quiz No. 58

1. Queen Victoria
2. One Pound
3. Hamilton Harbor
4. The Postmaster Stamp of 1948
5. Tennis
6. Cricket
7. 1975
8. Tall Ships
9. 50th
10. To Jamestown, Virginia, from Bermuda in 1610

Quiz No. 59

1. Traffic Signs
2. Pierre Laporte
3. Monsignor de Laval
4. 1976
5. Benjamin Franklin
6. Peace Bridge between Fort Erie, Ontario, and Buffalo, New York
7. Canadian Geese
8. Postal Code
9. 1979
10. Sports

Quiz No. 60

1. The Schooner "Bluenose"
2. King George V
3. Elizabeth and Margaret Rose
4. Destroyer
5. Alexander Graham Bell
6. John Cabot
7. Canada Goose
8. Chemical Industry
9. Post Horn and Globe
10. Mohawk Princess and poet

Quiz No. 61

1. 1904
2. Vasco Nunez de Balboa
3. Gen. George Washington Goethals
4. Boy Scouts
5. Gaillard Cut
6. Malaria
7. 29
8. Christopher Columbus
9. Pan American Clipper
10. S.S. Panama

Quiz No. 62

1. Basketball
2. Locomotive
3. Rhinoceros
4. Emperor Bokassa I
5. Bible
6. Mice
7. Centenary of International Telecommunications Union
8. Porter
9. A Scale
10. Charles de Gaulle

Quiz No. 63

1. Indian
2. Queen Victoria
3. Rubber Trees
4. Wild Elephants
5. Rice
6. Sri Lanka
7. First Prime Minister of Ceylon
8. Colombo
9. Malaria
10. Tea

Quiz No. 64

1. Pope Paul VI
2. A horse-drawn ambulance
3. Timber
4. Carrier Pigeon
5. United Nations
6. Skiing
7. Gandhi
8. Valparaiso Volunteer Lifeboat Service
9. Grapes
10. Antarctic

Quiz No. 65

1. Dr. Sun Yat-sen
2. President Chiang Kai-shek
3. Lincoln
4. Spiny Lobster
5. Basketball
6. Javelin Throwing
7. Squirrels
8. Little League Baseball
9. Tiger
10. Fireflies

Quiz No. 66

1. Fifteen
2. Fishing
3. Sailing
4. 200th
5. Historic Sailing Vessels
6. Princess Anne
7. Christmas Tree Ornaments
8. Apollo II
9. Official Stamps
10. Triangles

Quiz No. 67

1. Carp
2. Prague
3. Stamp Printing Works
4. Two
5. Vostok 2
6. Dog
7. Bicycling
8. 1979
9. Red, Blue or Green
10. J.F. Kennedy

Quiz No. 68

1. Benjamin Franklin
2. Honey Bee
3. Napoleon III
4. Washington
5. Paul Cezanne
6. Plane and Steamship
7. Dunkirk
8. A rural mailman on a bicycle
9. UNESCO
10. Clement Ader

Quiz No. 69

1. Lutheran Church
2. Konrad Duden's German Language Dictionary
3. NATO
4. Anne Frank
5. Nobel Peace Prize Winners
6. Ice Hockey
7. Konrad Adenauer
8. Thomas Aquinas
9. Calculator
10. Roswitha

Quiz No. 70

1. International Book Year
2. Friedrich Engels
3. Pope John XXIII
4. 50th Anniversary of Universal Women's Suffrage
5. Thurn and Taxis
6. John F. Kennedy
7. Heinrich Lubke
8. Saint George, Patron Saint of Boy Scouts
9. Gottlieb Daimler's Car of 1886
10. George C. Marshall

Quiz No. 71

1. Gold Coast
2. Africa
3. March 6, 1957
4. Lincoln Memorial
5. Red-Fronted Gazelle
6. The Introduction of Decimal Currency
7. Landing of Neil A. Armstrong on the Moon
8. The Wright Biplane
9. "Oh Come All Ye Faithful"
10. Metric System

Quiz No. 72

1. Charles, Prince of Wales
2. M. Gandhi
3. Charles Dickens
4. The Penny Black
5. Princess Anne and Captain Mark Phillips
6. Winston Chruchill
7. Sailboats and yachts
8. Stockton and Darlington Railway
9. Queen Elizabeth II
10. Primroses, Daffodils, Bluebells and Snowdrops

Quiz No. 73

1. One penny
2. Queen Victoria
3. Black
4. Lion
5. George VI
6. Queen Elizabeth II
7. William Shakespeare
8. Trinidad
9. Salvation Army
10. Supermarine Spitfire Fighters

Quiz No. 74

1. Bailiwick
2. English Channel
3. Thomas de la Rue
4. Hong Kong
5. Stained glass windows from Guernsey churches
6. Guernsey bull
7. Order of the Garter
8. Postal Bureau
9. Postage Due
10. Victor Hugo

Quiz No. 75

1. British Guiana
2. South America
3. 1966
4. Guyana Labor Union
5. Republic Day
6. Mohandas K. Gandhi
7. The Lord's Prayer
8. British Guiana
9. Namibia (Southwest Africa)
10. The introduction of new coinage

Quiz No. 76

1. British Crown Colony
2. Canton
3. Victoria
4. Ox
5. Scales
6. Chow
7. Cross Harbor Tunnel
8. George V
9. Queen Victoria Statue in Victoria Park
10. Carrier Pigeon

Quiz No. 77

1. Budapest Fair Buildings
2. Eleanor Roosevelt
3. International Red Cross
4. Soccer
5. Rose
6. Mining
7. Eight
8. Venus 4 landing on Venus
9. Endre Ady
10. Albrecht Durer

Quiz No. 78

1. Queen Victoria
2. East India Company
3. Elephants
4. Lotus Blossom
5. Boeing 707
6. Nehru
7. Buddha
8. 19th Century Postman
9. Lockheed Constellation
10. Dove

Quiz No. 79

1. Thomas Moore
2. St. Peter
3. Harp
4. The Irish Pavillion
5. Golden Key with CEPT Emblem
6. Pope John Paul II
7. Catherine McAuley
8. Girl Guides
9. The Centenary of Canadian Confederation
10. Wren, Great-Crested Grebe, Greenland White-Fronted Geese, Peregrine Falcon

Quiz No. 80

1. Harry Truman
2. Theodor Herzl
3. Chaim Weizmann
4. Haifa Bay
5. Running Stag
6. Typesetting
7. Izhak Ben-Zvi
8. Dancing
9. Tel Aviv
10. Ambulance

Quiz No. 81

1. Albert Einstein
2. 1979
3. La Scala
4. Volleyball
5. Titian
6. Rotary International
7. 400th
8. Leaning Tower of Pisa
9. Composer
10. Giuseppe Mazzini

Quiz No. 82

1. Caribbean Sea
2. George VI
3. 1962
4. Churchill
5. EXPO '67
6. Labor Day
7. Mongoose
8. Trumpet
9. Opening of Jamiaca's Earth Satellite Station
10. Olympic Rings

Quiz No. 83

1. Great Buddha of Kamakura
2. 1919 (Air Post Stamps)
3. Red Cross and Community Chest
4. International Year of the Child
5. Baseball
6. Dinosaur
7. Imperial Coach
8. Rugby
9. 1957 Stamp Week
10. Unzen National Park

Quiz No. 84

1. Douglas MacArthur
2. 1885
3. Dove
4. Syngman Rhee
5. The Express Train "Sam Chun Li"
6. Star of Bethlehem and Pine Cone
7. Hibiscus
8. Girl Scouts
9. Korea and Viet Nam
10. Yong Sik Hong

Quiz No. 85

1. Basutoland
2. Africa
3. Moshoeshoe I
4. Lord Baden Powell
5. Diamond Mining
6. Children climbing a tree
7. Botswana
8. World Rheumatism Year
9. 75th Anniversary of Powered Flight
10. Dances

Quiz No. 86

1. Joseph J. Roberts
2. Africa
3. William V.S. Tubman
4. John F. Kennedy and Abraham Lincoln
5. Dag Hammarskjold
6. Discus Throwing
7. Triangles
8. Statue of Liberty
9. Martin Luther King, Jr.
10. Japan

Quiz No. 87

1. Julius Caesar on Denarious c. 44 B.C.
2. Archery
3. Great Spotted Woodpecker
4. Brown Trout
5. 1852
6. Flowers
7. Mosel
8. Multiple airplanes
9. Winston Churchill
10. Occupation semi-postals

Quiz No. 88

1. Francisco (Pancho) Villa
2. Mayan
3. Marco Polo
4. John F. Kennedy
5. Paricutin
6. Piano Keyboard and Lara's signature
7. Penny Black of 1840
8. U Thant
9. Beethoven
10. Tire treads

Quiz No. 89

1. Triangle
2. 1950
3. Dr. Albert Schweitzer
4. Franklin D. Roosevelt
5. 1956
6. Pius XI and Pius XII
7. Henry Ford
8. Kennedy and Nixon
9. Dachshunds
10. Sardinia, France and Monaco

Quiz No. 90

1. William III
2. Wilhelmina
3. Mining
4. Queen Juliana and Prince Bernhard
5. Tennis
6. Belgium, Netherlands and Luxembourg
7. Poet
8. Franz Hals
9. Politicans
10. Curacao, Netherlands Indies and Surinam

Quiz No. 91

1. 1862
2. New Post Office at Managua
3. Rowland Hill
4. Cardinal Spellman
5. Pele
6. Anastasio Somoza
7. Balloon
8. St. Peter
9. James McDivitt and Edward White
10. Gustavo Diaz Ordaz of Mexico and Rene Schick of Nicaragua

Quiz No. 92

1. Water lilies
2. People and a punched card
3. Boats
4. Founder of the International Red Cross
5. Roald Amundsen
6. Olav V
7. Oslo University
8. Edward Grieg
9. The 20th anniversary of liberation from the Germans
10. King Haakon VII

Quiz No. 93

1. 1946
2. He was executed
3. Manuel L. Quezon
4. Eisenhower
5. Adolpho Lopez Mateos
6. 1966
7. Leyte
8. Fairchild FD-2
9. Bull
10. Bicycle

Quiz No. 94

1. The Warsaw Pact
2. Rowland Hill
3. George Washington
4. Children's Television Programs
5. Chickens
6. Chopin
7. Eagle
8. Tadeusz Kosciusko
9. Eleanor Roosevelt
10. Kayaks

Quiz No. 95

1. Italy
2. Christopher Columbus
3. Abraham Lincoln
4. Duryea
5. Dante Alighieri
6. Walt Disney
7. Wright Brothers
8. Red Cross of Italy
9. Glider
10. Melvin Jones

Quiz No. 96

1. Soccer
2. Austria
3. Jose San Martin and Simon Bolivar
4. Alexander Graham Bell
5. Goldsmiths
6. Bull
7. John XXIII
8. St. Peter
9. Carlos I of Spain
10. To distribute historical publications by Diego Castell

Quiz No. 97

1. Herring
2. Gustav VI Adolf
3. Stockholm
4. New Year's Eve
5. Coats of Arms
6. St. Bridget
7. Labor Party leader and Prime Minister
8. Table Tennis
9. The "Wasa"
10. Jenny Lind

Quiz No. 98

1. Medieval postal couriers
2. Women's Army Auxiliary
3. Geneva and Zurich
4. Trains
5. Alpine herdsmen
6. Barber
7. Dandelion
8. A dirigible
9. Swiss National Philatelic Exhibition at Zurich
10. Bacteriologist

Quiz No. 99

1. 1951
2. One dollar
3. An ear of wheat
4. Three and eight cents
5. General Assembly
6. The Scales of Justice
7. A child at a blackboard
8. U.N. Headquarters
9. Marc Chagall
10. Henrik Starcke

Quiz No. 100

1. 1929
2. Pius XI
3. St. Paul of the Cross
4. Praying Women
5. 1933
6. St. Peter
7. Postage Due
8. Astronomer
9. Four
10. Papal Arms

A Word About the American Philatelic Society

The American Philatelic Society, founded in 1886, is the oldest and largest national organization of stamp collectors in the United States. Its many thousands of active members span this country and more than 100 foreign nations. It is not necessary to be an advanced collector or wealthy specialist to attain APS membership and join the more than 53,000 others who already have done so.

National headquarters of the organization, which houses the American Philatelic Research Library as well as the APS central and editorial offices and sales division, is located in State College, Pennsylvania.

The American Philatelic Society publishes *The American Philatelist,* a monthly journal that has grown to become the largest of its type in the world. Authoritative articles covering every phase of philately, together with the latest news of the hobby and reliable advertising, make it a world leader. Regular features include worldwide new issues, new discoveries, columns on the practical aspects of the hobby, and how-to-do-it pieces provided by the outstanding philatelic writers of this country and the world.

An important and rapidly growing service to APS members is in the field of philatelic education. In cooperation with The Pennsylvania State University, APS has sponsored a series of philatelic correspondence courses that have far exceeded early optimistic expectations of usage by the stamp-collecting public. First courses deal with beginning philately (one course each for youths and adults) and intermediate aspects of the hobby. Further, more detailed courses are planned for the near future. An annual week-long seminar on philately is conducted by APS each summer in State College. Other approaches to philatelic education are in various stages of development.

The APS Sales Division operates as a non-profit activity of the Society, enabling members to sell stamps at member-designated prices and to acquire additions to their collections at clearly stated, reasonable costs. Members may receive, on request, sales circuits of specific countries with no obligation other than to forward the circuits to others as directed by a circuit route sheet. With this fully insured service, choice stamps with total values in the millions of dollars are available to all members.

All-risk stamp insurance for the protection of stamp collections is another of the services offered to APS members. This service is available to members residing in the United States and Canada. Detailed information about this broad, low-priced program is sent to all new members when they are admitted to membership.

The APS Expert Committee of more than 140 outstanding philatelic specialists, in cooperation with the American Stamp Dealers' Association professional panel, renders skilled opinions regarding the genuineness or identity of stamps and covers. A small fee is charged for each item submitted.

APS offers its members a free translation service in almost all major languages. For normal letters and short statements, there is no charge other than a return, stamped envelope. For articles or lengthy communications, a minimum fee is charged.

The number of local stamp clubs in this country and abroad that are APS Chapters continues to increase; they now total more than 700. Also, more than eighty specialist stamp societies are Affiliates of the American Philatelic Society.

At its annual conventions and spring meetings conducted in major cities across the nation, APS presents the finest in philatelic exhibitions. These displays of the world's superior stamps, postal stationery, and other interesting items of philatelic research afford a liberal education for members and non-members alike. The exhibitions also allow members to gain information and suggestions for improving their own collections. The APS also sponsors the annual "World Series of Philately," wherein grand award winners from the nation's top exhibitions compete to become the Champion of Champions.

The services of the American Philatelic Research Library are available to all APS members by mail, and to all others by inter-library loan. Books may be borrowed from its extensive reference collection, and photocopies may be obtained. The Library publishes the quarterly *Philatelic Literature Review*.

Information on membership in the American Philatelic Society, as well as about any of the individual services noted above, is available by writing to APS, American Philatelic Building, P.O. Box 8000, State College, PA 16801.